LUMINA TAROT

LUMINA
TAROT

Lauren Aletta

Let your intuition guide you

ROCKPOOL

A Rockpool book
PO Box 252
Summer Hill
NSW 2130
Australia

rockpoolpublishing.com
Follow us! **f** 🅾 rockpoolpublishing
Tag your images with #rockpoolpublishing

First published in 2015
This edition published in 2024 by Rockpool Publishing
ISBN: 9781922786289

Design and typesetting by Sara Lindberg, Rockpool Publishing
Illustrated by Tegan Swyny
Edited by Rebecca Sutherland

Printed and bound in China
10 9 8 7 6 5 4 3 2 1

CONTENTS

✦

INTRODUCTION

Lumina Tarot was birthed through my desire for a tarot deck that had a modern yet classic style. When I couldn't find one, I was inspired to create one! The old adage 'create what you wish existed' awakened a sense of purpose within me, and just like The Fool I set off on a creative journey to bring to life a soulful tarot deck with an earthy yet magical vibe that would empower the user to trust in themselves.

Lumina Tarot is a tool for you to reach the places of yourself that are at times hard to touch. It's not so much a divination tool as it is a mirror, offering self-exploration, reflection and confirmation. *Lumina* invites you to see yourself in new ways, calling you to come back into your own knowing, where you can feel the stirrings of your soul's essence guiding you forward. Let go of your judgements and preconceived ideas and move into the waters of your natural intuitive ability. Lean into this feeling, for it is from this place that you are able to unfold your own mystery.

WORKING WITH THE CARDS

The universe is alive and listening. When you take time to intentionally connect and play with the cards, the universe is ready to work with and through you, guiding and supporting you with the answers you've been seeking.

Some tips

The universe responds to your dominant intent. This means the intention you hold for yourself, a particular situation, or how you wish to experience your life is a vibration you emit. Your vibrations are clearly and continuously communicating to your surroundings (and the universe) what you desire and what you expect.

Take a moment or two to settle into a centred place and clearly determine what your question is. If you cannot articulate the question, that's okay – allow your question to be expressed in a clear feeling.

Your intuition and internal guidance system

The universe responds to your dominant intent to support you in actualising what you are seeking through your intuition and internal guidance system.

Your internal guidance system (IGS) exists between you and your soul. It is there to support you in living the fullest, freest, most joyous life you possibly can. It can be described as your internal compass: the part of you that lets you know how far away you are from yourself and how you can navigate back to centre.

Your internal guidance system translates, integrates and understands the depth and breadth of who you are at a soul level, while also understanding the complexities of being human. It's there to provide guidance to propel you forward, so you can express and experience your deep desires and heal whatever may need to be healed. It knows how to guide you from A to B with the least resistance and greatest pleasure.

Your IGS is also why, when you look outside of yourself for guidance, you often feel even more confused or stifled. No one can decide what is appropriate or inappropriate for you, because that is between you and your higher self (or soul).

While your IGS is the junction point between your soul self and your human self, your intuition is the way that your IGS communicates information and insight. Pay attention to the very first impressions that come as soon as you pull a card. Watch for pictures, inspired ideas, gut feelings or heart flutters! The closer your attention, the more depth of insight you are able to receive.

Get centred and clear

Tune your thoughts and energy for an intuitive play session.

If you're ready for some clear guidance, get centred and clear. If you're feeling confused, settle yourself into a state of neutrality and softness. If you are ready for love, or to know the next step, be clear about that in your energy and thoughts.

When you express a desire or wish, you send energy outward, and the universe will respond accordingly. The insight you'll receive will be reflective of your energy. So get centred!

Tarot Journal

A CARD A DAY

A beautiful practice is to pull a card a day for a month. This allows you to notice any running themes playing out in your life, as well as heightening your intuitive and reflective abilities.

Each morning, not long after rising, take a moment to connect in with yourself, ask a question if necessary, then pull a card from the facedown deck. Give the card your attention and observe any initial thoughts, impressions, feelings and images that spring to mind.

You may want to hold the intention of asking what the clear message or word is behind the card. Jot the impressions and guidance down – it can simply be a sentence or two.

Pay attention to any highlights or clear messages throughout your daily activity that may relate back to the card's insights and guidance.

NEW MOON AND FULL MOON INSIGHT

If you are keen to explore and include moon rituals in your life, using your cards at the new and full moon is a wonderful way to gather insight and build energy and momentum around a desire, and also receive guiding direction around how to navigate forward.

New Moon

This is a time for intention setting.

Tune in and listen to what you are being called to move into. Pull a card and receive the guiding message that will prompt your intention. If you are seeking more directional support, hold your intention as a feeling in your body. Then ask these questions and pull a card for each:

+ Where am I now?
+ Where am I moving towards?
+ What can I do to move towards manifesting my intention?

You may feel you need to pull more than one card for this last question.

Enjoy the fullness of this experience ... allow all the energy of your intention to flow into you.

Full Moon

A time of release and action.

The full moon is a time of actioning any leads that have been generated by your new moon intention, or, if you have found your new moon intention was not aligned or appropriate for where you are right now, it's about releasing it with love.

With your intention in mind, ask the following, while pulling a card for each question:

+ What do I need to know right now?
+ What action do I need to take?
+ What do I need to surrender?

Let go of whatever you are being called to release.

CHAKRA SPREAD

Slip into a quiet receiving space and connect with each of your chakras, starting from the base chakra and working up. Allow the energy to guide you in pulling a card from the deck and then intuitively receive the guidance the visual prompts of the card give you.

Pay attention to your:

✦ First thoughts
✦ First feelings
✦ Any clear intuitions or messages

If you feel there is a particular chakra that requires attention, you may like to attune yourself and explore questions like:

✦ What is this chakra processing?
✦ What does it wish for me to know?
✦ How can I support it?
✦ Is there anything I need to heal?

Trust yourself, your soul knowing and your body.

INSIGHTS AND ARCHETYPES

Major arcana

The major arcana takes you on a 22-card hero's journey, from beginning to end, symbolic of a soul's internal growth. Each major arcana card is an archetype of energy we all hold within ourselves, that we naturally experience as we walk the adventure of our soul.

The journey of the major arcana begins with The Fool (marked as 0), moving to the card of completion, The World (marked 21). The major arcana are heavily weighted and highly energetic cards of the tarot, so pay attention to how you feel when they appear in a spread.

Minor arcana

The minor arcana are the remaining 56 cards, made up of four suits of 14 cards each: Wands, Cups, Swords and Pentacles. The minor arcana marks progress, giving guidance, insight and support along the four elemental paths that make up our world. They add depth to a reading, building on the strong themes and energies of a spread.

Each suit of the minor arcana ranges from ace to 10 – a journey of inspiration, possibility, opportunity, challenge, endings and success – followed by the court cards, which can represent people in your life (near or far), or qualities you possess.

SUITS AND ELEMENTS

WANDS: Fire

The suit of Wands is all fiery passion, ambition, creativity, determination and inspiration! Wands often mirror what is at our core, highlighting elements of our mind and ego along with the spiritual aspects of our consciousness. They represent what you do during your day: what you live for, what you're passionately seeking. Their shadow side is one of illusions, impulsiveness, brashness, disinterest, arrogance and egotistical behaviour.

+ **Symbolic animal:** Fox
+ **Fire signs:** Leo, Sagittarius, Aries
+ **Personality traits:** Highly energetic, passionate, inspirational, full of action, charming, spiritually driven and cutting edge in their ideas. Can be aloof, fickle and revengeful.

CUPS: Water

The suit of Cups is all about emotion, intuition and fluidity: creativity, fantasy, imagination, romanticism and dreams. Cups highlight our relationships, including the relationship we have with ourselves, communicating to us about love, matters of the heart and making heart-based decisions. The shadow side of Cups can be indulging excessively in emotion, or being emotionally repressed, depressed or disengaged.

- ✦ **Symbolic animal:** Serpent
- ✦ **Water signs:** Pisces, Cancer, Scorpio
- ✦ **Personality traits:** Artistic feelers, often highly creative, leading with the heart, guided by feelings. Can be overly emotional, ungrounded and lack logic.

SWORDS: Air

Swords, representative of Air, are about swift action, mental astuteness, power, oppression and conflict. The suit of Swords is focused around mental consciousness, intellect, attitude and beliefs, and how these create your world. The Swords family use their minds to overcome challenges or to create opportunity. However, they can use their cleverness in manipulative ways.

- ✦ **Symbolic animal:** Hawk
- ✦ **Air signs:** Aquarius, Libra, Gemini
- ✦ **Personality traits:** Thoughtful, quick-witted, clever, logical minds, understanding the world through analysis. Can be ruthless, confrontational and closed to new ideas.

PENTACLES: Earth

Pentacles represent our external, material world: our finances, property, work or business. This suit understands that a flourishing external world extends from a flourishing internal world. It is a suit of manifestation, prosperity and the realisation of dreams. A very warm and grounded suit, Pentacles highlight our self-esteem and self-worth, and how these create our world. Their shadow side deals with soulless materialism.

+ **Symbolic animal:** Bear
+ **Earth signs:** Taurus, Virgo, Capricorn
+ **Personality traits:** Down to earth, generous, warm, practical, enjoy pleasurable experiences, often deeply connected to the Earth, business minds. Can be greedy, possessive and materialistic.

Reversals

A card pulled upside down can denote the underside, unseen or shadow side of a situation.

It is up to you if you wish to incorporate a reversed or shadow aspect of a card into your readings. Do what is best for the way you work.

Not all reversed cards will represent a shadow aspect. Trust your immediate feeling and sense. You may find that upright card meanings are more relevant.

MAJOR ARCANA

0 ✦ THE FOOL

Going your own way

The beginning of a journey. What you're embarking on may seem reckless and foolish. Butterflies fill your stomach and you may ask yourself, 'What am I doing?' It may feel like you are reaching for the stars, yet you're filled with an unexplainable knowing that this is the right way to go. Innocent, naive and with your heart full of light, you step forward into the unknown, listening to your own drum beat. This journey will take courage, determination and independence.

The spark of life! The Fool is the ultimate beginning and can appear after setbacks or endings. It often marks the beginning of a significant period, not only in your material surrounds but also within. It can feel like your mind, body and spirit have aligned and you're now moving forward as a new and increasingly powerful being. Do not worry that you may not know how to do what you are being called to do: you will overcome this along the way. This is where you discover and come to know who you truly are.

The Fool may represent the beginning of a new relationship, job, travelling adventure, study or business. Whatever it is you are being called to do, do it your way.

Trust your intuition. Be spontaneous. Follow your inner being. Beauty and wonder await you.

REVERSED

A message of caution. Are you being too reckless? Are you acting without thought of consequence? Have you put yourself in a situation where you're being taken advantage of?

Keep following your own lead, but be wise about it. Adventuring without awareness only creates danger.

This may also represent blocks, false starts or beliefs holding you back from your true potential. Be daring, but not impulsive or immature.

I ✦ THE MAGICIAN

Alchemy

You are gathering tools and harnessing your creative powers to powerfully and actively manifest your bold vision. This is about implementing what you have observed in order to commence a new life cycle reflective of your unique self. You have moved from the idea of doing something your own way to now actually doing it! This is a highly dynamic process: pure magic in motion, pure alchemy. This is the time to think outside the box and test the waters. Small seeds grow, so start!

The Magician is charismatic and powerful because he believes in his vision and himself. When a person is completely aligned and connected to themselves, doors open. People watch with intrigue and wonder, and will inevitably get behind a person willing to give their all.

Do not fear your own power and potential. Soften your edges, step back from conditioning. Unleash the bright and boundless energy within you.

REVERSED

A reversed Magician may indicate that you hold a great many skills and talents that are lying dormant, often due to your own fear. You are being encouraged to explore yourself and your uniqueness. It may also mean that you are aware of your abilities – especially your spiritual and intuitive abilities – but you're not using them to support and serve you. Why are you holding yourself back? What are you afraid of? Now is the time to make change.

If you have allowed yourself to be taken to great yet illusionary heights, bring yourself back down to reality. Your power is potent only when grounded. Bring your attention within.

The reversed Magician may also represent a conman. This character is highly personable and engaging, yet they are untrustworthy, manipulative and cunning.

II ✦ THE HIGH PRIESTESS

Studying your wisdom within

You are increasingly beginning to look within for direction and guidance, rather than seeking input from others. Everything is becoming clearer to you. It is as though you are able to see through the veil of illusions and access the point where truth and light reside. Slowly, you are beginning to work with your own essence, flowing with your currents of inspiration and energy and accepting what is and what has been, knowing that it has led you here and will take you where you are going.

This is a card of esoteric knowledge that cannot be learned by book but instead is experienced and felt. It is the union of seen and unseen forces, generating light. By coming back to the illumination of self, you are able to serve yourself and the world.

Acknowledge your shadows, radiate your light. Begin to look at the world through the universe's eyes. Pay attention to subtle messages you are given in your dreams, waking visions and through daily signs. If you are experiencing problems or challenges, step back from reacting and look at the situation through fresh and connected eyes. Live the mystery.

REVERSED

If you look at a problem head on, you do not see it for what it is, nor what it offers. You are concentrating your energies on the outer world: it is time to step back and seek counsel from your internal reserves. Listen to your inner voice – it sees life from all perspectives and holds your highest interest.

For those cut off from intuition, this may be encouragement to reconnect. Set down your stubbornness and move back to being whole. It is far harder to reach the heights you wish for while only being half of who you are.

III ✦ THE EMPRESS

Flourishing growth

Powerful feminine beauty is pushing up through your fertile inner worlds, offering warmth and strength. You are accessing The Empress within: a majestic and magical force who thrives on aligned living, grounding, connection and appreciation of the beauty around you. A continual sense of fulfilment energises you, allowing you to share this wealth with others. Your creations and connections blossom under your fingertips.

You have entered a period of creativity, giving you access to parts of yourself and the universe you had only imagined. Observe and explore these dynamic and feminine forces.

The Empress is a ruler superior to all queens; an earth mother and goddess, all things spring from her love and kindness. She holds very little physical wealth: her abundance comes from the respect and reverence of those she serves.

Recognise that you already have everything you need, connect with nature and loved ones and embrace the powerful yin energy within. Explore your own mother energy and the mother energy surrounding you, from your matriarchal line to your kindred sisters and Gaia herself.

REVERSED

A reversed Empress alludes to disconnection from your personal power and vibrancy due to investing so much of yourself in others, with little rejuvenation. Emotionally and spiritually caring for the people in your life has left you burnt out, stunting your creative fire. You may feel exhausted, depressed, frustrated and bitter. It is time to come back to your core. Spend time in nature and in solace. Make room for playfulness and sensuality and find avenues for creative expression. Invite freshness in.

A disconnect from yourself may also be due to a sense of something being missing. Continually yearning will only perpetuate and expand this energy of lack and loss. Listen to your inner voice. You are always being guided and supported.

IV ✦ THE EMPEROR

Personal authority and responsibility

It is time to reign over your own life! You are being called to create structure and stability through your own means and on your own terms within your world. It is time to stand strong within yourself, owning who you are and what you represent, bold in your visions and life rules. It is vital to have authority over your own life before you contribute to others. You may be beginning to see significant growth, momentum and respect for your offerings within an organisation or your own business.

Others are recognising your knowledge and ability to cut through chaos and create order.

The Emperor is the masculine to The Empress's feminine. He is authoritative, decisive and stable; loving and compassionate, yet firm and protective. He is a strong and fair leader who is able to reach clarity and implement strategy. At his best he acts in love, holding the desire to improve the lives of those around him. When he is misaligned he can be rigid, stubborn and overbearing.

REVERSED

You may have allowed your thoughts to be misguided, falling into low vibrational territory. Amplifying this energy outwardly potentially leads to frustration, anger and loss. While you can sense you're out of balance, you may feel unsure how to restore order and calm, within and without. It would be wise to temporarily step back.

This card may also appear if you are feeling controlled and dominated by others, be it within a workplace or relationship. You are seeking freedom or space, as they are not aligning with your core values and beliefs. You may have nonconformist ideals needing to be expressed. It is time to stand up and assert yourself. Complaining will solve nothing. Neither will allowing yourself to be downtrodden.

V ✦ THE HIEROPHANT

A guiding authority

The Hierophant represents authority outside of traditional structures. Often this means exploring esoteric and spiritual practices or alternative lifestyle choices, or choosing to disengage from some of the beliefs that have captured you. Perhaps following mainstream guidelines has left you feeling empty and unsatisfied, and you are sensing an emerging interest or energy within that you are desiring to harness and understand. You are seeking deeper insight and confirmation, calling you to reach out to a mentor who has walked and is living the path you are considering. You are ready to expand your personal knowledge and undertake a more authentic path for your soul.

The Hierophant is a mentor, guiding authority, shaman or philosopher who provides support. This card may come to you at a time when you are ready to expand your knowledge in a particular area or step out to live a more aligned life. It is important you do not limit yourself: stay open to new ideas and principles. You never know how they will support you on your venture forward.

Now is a beautiful time to explore alchemy, ceremonies, rituals, rites of passage and new learnings though workshops.

REVERSED

You may have been running on autopilot and making life choices based upon seeking the approval of others, rather than from the aligned guidance of your own heart. You may feel fearful that if you make soul-based decisions you will be rejected for having a unique perspective on life. It is time to acknowledge your own self and begin to step further into who you are and who you are becoming.

Do not let your past failures stop you from believing in yourself.

VI ✦ THE LOVERS

The love of choice through the adventure

The Lovers card is all about choice: the power we have in the love we invite into our lives. This stretches from romantic and intimate love to loving oneself and one's life. This card represents that you are calling in aligned vibrations of love and union, whether it is that you are ready for a romantic union that reflects your soul's desires, or simply desiring fun company. Receiving The Lovers suggests uplifting and radiant, heart-surging feelings of connection and mutual appreciation.

Perhaps you have reached a place within yourself where you are loving and accepting of your journey and your soul. This can feel like a spiritual experience of the deepest kind of love, leaving you in full appreciation and gratitude for your life.

This may also be confirmation that a decision or new direction you are considering embarking upon will lead to fulfilment and abundance.

Love comes in an array of forms. Now is a wonderful time to ask yourself how you want to feel and what kind of love you desire across the depth and breadth of your life. Make choices that are your own truth.

REVERSED

Reversed, this card is one of encouragement. It may be that you need to come into love and acceptance of yourself first, before you pursue a romantic partner in your life. Remember, we draw in the vibration reflective of ourselves.

This card reversed may also represent infidelity, dishonesty, lust or misaligned energies. Take a step back from the situation and turn within. What are you choosing not to see?

Another important question to ask is: where are you not allowing yourself to receive love?

VII ✦ THE CHARIOT

Align your energy

The Chariot represents your inner strength, confidence and willpower. It is a card of action and momentum, calling you to focus yourself and be disciplined and determined in bringing your vision and desires to life. Summon all of your energy and intent towards not only your physical journey but also your spiritual one, to achieve the kind of fulfilment you seek.

The Chariot is your aligned energies. The more you are able to stabilise your vibration, the greater the energy and momentum you will create. From a place of inspiration and vision, you can ride on the backs of wild horses to reach the heights of success. Challenges and obstacles will be a source of opportunity and growth, developing additional strength and wisdom within.

This card may come as confirmation that you are indeed co-creating with the universe in a dynamic and powerful way towards your end goals. Enjoy the adventure you are on!

This could also be a warning to keep your eyes on the prize. Pay attention and commit to the whole experience as an awakened being. You are being given what you are projecting. So, what are you projecting? Where does your focus lie?

REVERSED

Have you been driving yourself too hard? It may be time to pull back and reflect. Perhaps you have slipped into overdrive, restricting flow and working from a place of resistance and push.

This card reversed may also represent confusion and misaligned thoughts. You may be darting from one place to the next, seeking a solution. Come back within yourself and explore what it is that you desire. Practise attuning your energies to a feeling that is reflective of your being. From here, clarity and inner knowing will be able to lead you forward.

VIII ✦ JUSTICE

Conscious awareness within decisions

This is a powerful card that speaks of seeking balance between your higher and lower bodies, ensuring that your choices are in harmony with the greater good. You are being called to take responsibility for your thoughts, words and deeds.

The Justice card reflects truth, honesty and fairness, and extending these ethics towards oneself and others. Perhaps there are decisions to make. You may be at a crossroads and are being called to make choices that require conscious awareness. Consider all aspects of the situation while looking within at your own values. There is not necessarily a wrong or right choice, simply a cause and effect. Remain objective at this time and use your internal compass for guidance. When you are aligned in your own truth and love, your decision will reflect this.

On a more practical level, Justice may appear regarding a legal matter or personal situation. Do not allow yourself to be exploited by others and do not be fooled into believing you can exploit others without an equal return of energy.

Consider the ideology of karma.

REVERSED

Are you acting irresponsibly and making rash decisions, ignorant of the potential outcomes? Or perhaps you are simply putting your head in the sand and ignoring the consequences. You are being called to be mindful of the domino effect you are setting in motion. When you are still within yourself, are the decisions you are making a true reflection of you and your desires?

Take time to reflect and gain perspective. While it may be satisfying momentarily to act impulsively, you could regret it later.

This card reversed may also be reflective of obstacles or challenges you are currently dealing with. Stay within your own integrity. Truth, fairness and justice will be served.

IX ✦ THE HERMIT

Illuminate your heart and mind

The Hermit counsels you to follow your own path, allowing your heart and mind to be illuminated by your soul and your natural connection with the universe. You may be feeling lost, or have begun to recognise shifts within yourself asking to move in a new direction. Withdraw from your regular activities and pull back on socialising where you can. Create a space where you can hear the answers you are being gifted.

You are being asked to authentically develop your own path and unfurl yourself in a natural and aligned way.

If you are being pressured to make decisions, it may be wise to hold off if possible. Slow down: be observant of your own natural cycles and move *with* them rather than against them. You are seeking the deeper answers to life's mysteries. Surrender judgement towards yourself and others, and simply be.

It is the perfect time to explore meditation, yoga or any practice that turns your awareness within. You have the power to light your own path, you do not need the guidance of others.

REVERSED

The reversed Hermit may ask why you continue to deny the calling of your own truth. You are walking in the direction of what you think you should do, rather than what you know you should do. Do not allow yourself to be influenced by the external world and the opinions of others. Trust your innate wisdom; it will never lead you astray.

This card reversed may also be acknowledging that, while pulling back from the world to create solitude and stillness can be helpful, too much withdrawal is harmful. Do not isolate yourself. You are you, but you are also all the family, friends and beauty around you.

X ✦ THE WHEEL OF FORTUNE

Cycles of life: birth, death, rebirth

You are being reminded of the continual flow of life and to move with it rather than against it. There will always be deterioration and death, followed by stillness, then the warm, fresh growth of birth and new life. Night follows day and Spring follows Winter. You are exactly the same.

Positive and exciting change is afoot; in fact, change is always afoot in some form. It is wise not to resist this. This card may also speak of your chakras, encouraging you to attune yourself to their wisdom. This will allow you to process information with confidence and ease.

Do not simply stand still and accept what life delivers. You are far more powerful than that. Be the course creator! Intentionally move the spinning wheel to the beat of your own heart's guidance. You may be at a pivotal point in your life, filled with possibility or feeling uncertain and fearful. Expand yourself outward. See things from a higher perspective and stay connected to the feeling of your own truth. Know that wherever you are on the wheel, it will pass.

REVERSED

Your outlook needs adjustment. You are out of sync and it is causing havoc within yourself and your life. This may present in a low sense of disconnection, fogginess or confusion as to why your life feels the way it does.

This card reversed appears as a gentle nudge of support, telling you your alignment with yourself is out. It is not that you shouldn't feel this array of emotions, but your cultivation of a disharmonious energy is preventing the growth and change you are seeking.

Things may be drawing to a close. This is normal. Look ahead to what will follow. Do not resist change.

XI + STRENGTH

Inner strength of spirit

Leading with your heart and building your life from the core strength, compassion and courage you possess will lead you to achieve all your soul's desires. You are transcending your attachments to fear and fickle emotions, and relying more heavily on your own internal knowing and integrity.

Soon you will see how life works for you. Living in this way takes practise, but it transforms. Trust in your instinctual knowledge and act from love. You have what it takes to tame the beasts within yourself and others with gentle kindness, understanding and truth. You are accessing your own confidence and relying on your intuition and spiritual wisdom more and more, trusting in the journey and holding conviction for what you know is right.

Accept and forgive your own and others' flaws. Embrace both yours and others' mistakes. From this position you are able to influence others in a connected and conscious way. A true leader shines from within, creating a soft place for others to feel safe and held, no matter their armour.

A time of internal power – whatever task, dream or challenge is at hand, move it with your strength.

REVERSED

Are you feeling inadequate and weak? Or are you trying to make change, but with force, aggression and manipulation? The reversed Strength card is asking you to look deeper within yourself. Access the rich, ancient sunlight that exists within the core of your being to navigate the challenges at hand.

Do not doubt your power and strength and do not give it away. You have all the skills and vibrational qualities within you to create positive change for yourself and others. With courage and determination you can turn the situation around. Let the magic begin!

XII ✦ THE HANGED MAN

Release expectation to reduce confusion

The Hanged Man appears when you are feeling suspended before an action or decision. There is often the sense that something higher is calling you to pause in time and really see. This card may appear to you in relation to a decision, or in regard to your current perspective on yourself and life. You are being asked to elevate yourself a little higher and look at what is going on with a fresh perspective. This may feel uncomfortable at first, but the answers to the questions you have been asking lie within this pregnant pause.

At times the Hanged Man will be calling you to make what seems like a sacrifice. But the larger aspects of your soul know that you are consciously choosing to flow with a creative force that will achieve the greater good.

Let go of whatever it is you are holding on to. Release this energy and invite in what the universe is offering you. In this state, your awareness is at full bloom.

REVERSED

Are you experiencing a loss of faith because you are feeling stagnant? See this as a clear message to stay connected to the core feeling of trust and alignment as best you can. This pause is necessary for unseen synchronicities, events and changes to align. Yet, you must be active in this process! Stop holding yourself back.

This card reversed can also be a clear message that while you continue to wait for things to shift and change, the standstill will continue. You are the catalyst here and you are being called to act. Follow the internal guidance you are being given and step forward. Let go of the beliefs that are prolonging this limbo.

XIII + DEATH

XIII + DEATH

The transition and transformation of life

What was once vibrant and energised naturally dissipates and falls away. Death is the word we use to symbolise this life process.

Something in your life is beginning to fall away and transform. At first this will feel like loss. Sadness and the instinct to cling to what energy remains is natural, yet nothing can hold back death. Flow with this energy of transition and transformation. The fleshy life of what once was always leaves lessons and structure to build new life upon. It is up to you to see it this way.

You may be faced with a major life phase coming to an end. Whether it be an aspect of yourself, your career or a relationship, honour this time of ending. Celebrate what you have been gifted. Lean back on your soul's guidance when you need strength and courage, and ready yourself for what is to come. New beginnings are afoot, bringing with them exciting change and renewed vitality and vibrancy.

The Death card is not to be feared, but embraced.

REVERSED

You may be closed off to new life and opportunity because you have not embraced, made peace with and let go of a pivotal phase in your life. You may be clinging to something that is no longer there. This is causing you pain and hardship. Walk through the coals of this fire and release what is needed so you are able to move forward and birth new life again.

If you are on the brink of a transition phase, let go and look within. To attempt to run from it will only exhaust you physically, emotionally and spiritually. Move with your cycles. Beauty and new adventures await you.

XIV ✦ TEMPERANCE

Balance and harmony in life

Temperance is the card of practice. It appears when you are consciously choosing to harmonise yourself and your life to create balance and order. This is a very fluid process. When we reach higher into ourselves and our connection to the cosmos, we are able to seamlessly make the changes needed to feel like ourselves. If you have felt inspired to move back into alignment with yourself and your purpose, see this card as confirmation that you are being guided. Listen to the feelings, inner knowing and direction you have been given.

This card may come as you are stepping towards creating something potent and powerful. Yet you are not in a hurry, because you understand that you are simply the vessel for what is moving through you. Harmony and balance are foundational for success. Move with the energy that is being gifted to you through each phase of the process.

This card may also appear if you are experiencing difficulty or challenge in your life. You may be enduring anger, frustration, excess or lack. Come back to your own centre. Your inner being knows how to manoeuvre this situation with harmony, balance and ease.

REVERSED

Reversed Temperance indicates disharmony and conflict in your life. Now is a beautiful time to balance it. Temperance reversed may also appear as warning guidance that walking a particular path will lead to imbalance and disharmony.

Look at the grander vision of your life. You may be feeling out of balance due to small thinking, but once you allow the fullness of what is possible, you will feel aligned. Expect a delicious surge of energy and power to follow.

XV ✦ THE DEVIL

Warning to be watchful

Your natural state is to be vibrant and happy, full of inspiration and joy. Yet part of the human experience is pain, lack, addiction, entrapment and dis-ease. Often we are unaware that it is our very own self that invites and accepts the opposite of what we know and desire. The Devil represents our fear and disconnection, which often leads to self-destructive and self-sabotaging behaviours.

Where are you feeling trapped? Where are you sabotaging yourself, preventing you from achieving and receiving what you desire? It is a time for total honesty. Hide behind the scapegoat of others or excuses no longer. The despair and sense of hopelessness you may feel are only reflective of the stories you continue to buy into and make true.

Watch yourself. Do not be tempted by the stories your mind has become accustomed to telling. Rise above. You may wish to reconsider your course of action at this time.

REVERSED

Reversed, The Devil may indicate addiction, destruction, powerlessness, excessive force and control, recklessness, disconnection and harm. It may herald a situation coming to a head, where one can no longer hide behind the untruths, excuses and many guises they have been hiding behind. The awakening and realisation of the traps one has set for oneself has come. An unravelling or rock bottom must occur.

This card reversed may also symbolise the need to step back. You have become too attached and reliant on a person or item. Rise above your fear and move into a new space of self-reliance and trust. This may take time, but the benefits, great and small, will be immediate.

Finally, sometimes this card reversed can be seen as a clear passage. There is no risk of harm; you are free to move forward.

XVI ✦ THE TOWER

The crumbling of old paradigms

Destruction is in the air! Do not shy away. Stand up to the electricity of a storm and breathe in the freshness of life: exhale and let go of the decay and immorality of what once was.

The Tower appears when it seems as though your world is crumbling. Perhaps you've lost your job, your relationship is breaking down, or you can no longer view the world as you once did. Regardless, the momentum is building to a crescendo. As the structures of your internal and external worlds crumble, ask yourself, what do I really want? What does my heart desire? What no longer works for me? What do I need to let go of? What direction must I move towards?

You may be feeling overwhelmed, uncertain and insecure, especially if the change was unexpected. Do not step outside your power, for there is an awakening occurring within you and your world. Stagnant patterns of thinking and being are breaking up, gifting you the freedom to pursue your soul's desires and transform them into physical reality.

This is a card of personal breakthrough, where new worlds begin.

REVERSED

Are you attempting to alter the course of nature? Are you trying to resist the destruction of something within your life? In the process of resisting what will be, you are holding back the flourishing growth of yourself. Navigating through the breakdown of one's life may not be easy or joyful, but whatever is occurring now is pivotal.

It may also be that the fear of change is worse than what will actually occur. Begin to tune yourself to what feels good, rather than turning to your fears. Step towards your vision, even if it means stepping into the unknown.

XVII ✦ THE STAR

Inspiration ignites from within

You are surrounded by beauty! You have everything you need and all that you witness in your life has sprung from the creative divinity of your core. After a period of trials or difficulty you are opening yourself to healing, love and abundance. This is a period of magic and transformation. Everything may not be perfect, but you're no longer striving for perfection: you're seeking authenticity.

This is a time of inspiration, of listening to your innate nature. Be aware of how the universe is working with and through you, offering guidance in the form of physical sensations and synchronistic symbols. You are uncovering meaning, passion and purpose, allowing you to finally honour the person you are.

This is a card of renewed self-trust and self-esteem. Creativity abounds – you are seeing the world with bright and fresh eyes. Put this creativity and inspiration into action, making your life a work of art!

The Star may also highlight a spiritual mission.

REVERSED

The Star reversed implies that you may have lost faith in yourself or a situation. You may be looking for a sign to guide you. Rather than continuing to look for external signs, it may be time to turn inward. Access the goddess or god within. Take inspiration from the swirling energies inside, surround yourself with people and activities that inspire you and spend time in nature and meditation. Believe in your innate core!

This card reversed may also appear if you have lost drive and motivation. It is normal for the mundane ordinariness of life to at times steamroll inspiration, but it is your job to keep connected to yourself so that you may harness and introduce the next fresh element.

XVIII ✦ THE MOON

Intuitive insight for illumination

This is a card of intuitive and psychic strength. Messages are coming through your subconscious; it may be a period of heightened dreams and memories, clearing away blocks and confusion that have distorted your view.

The Moon can be a shadow card, illuminating the darker aspects of yourself. This is an opportunity to embrace these aspects, harnessing your shadow's power and using it to your advantage. Be illuminated by your underworld. Feel into your watery depths, as they will lead you to higher levels of understanding.

If you are ready to bring your dreams to life and intentionally make change, working with the moon will project powerful ripples of energy, communicating to the universe that you are ready to receive.

This card may also indicate that things aren't as they seem. You may be filled with insecurity and anxiety, unsure of who you are. Be cautious of making decisions in this time: you do not want to be deceived. It is time for you to extend yourself. Do not make decisions from your rational mind alone: lean into the guidance your intuition provides.

REVERSED

Emotional issues and self-doubt inhibit you. Confusion and depression may be high, and most of your self-talk is false or only surface level. The depth of insight your emotions wish to communicate to you surpasses what you are currently grasping. Dive deeper. Work through your fears, go into your inner world and access the illuminated gold that resides within.

This card may also signal a reprieve. You have done the hard work, embraced your darker aspects and are now coming out the other side to find you have a strong psychic and intuitive connection. Use your newfound strengths to your advantage and move forward with confidence.

XIX ✦ THE SUN

Radiate who you are, soak up life's rays

You are reaching a period in your life where you are able to shine! Light radiates from you: you are energised and vital and able to gift your light to those you encounter. The Sun is a card of warmth, blessings and success. You can really feel your own power and see the bright and grand vision of what makes you truly happy.

You may be beginning to recognise, explore and harness previously untapped or underdeveloped talents. It feels exciting and liberating to know that there are landscapes within you that remain untouched!

If you receive this card in the aftermath of tough times, take refuge in it. Know that enlightenment and energy are on their way to you. Stop holding yourself back and begin to shine! As soon as you start to emanate your own vibration you will be met with an abundance of energetic projection in return.

Take time to enjoy life. Get outside and play in nature. Count your blessings and know that the adventure you have embarked on will lead you to the fulfilment and success you yearn for.

REVERSED

Do not force optimism. If you are finding that your efforts are being blocked or that you're having to force positivity, it may be an indication that you have fallen off your axis. This push towards positivity may actually prevent you from falling back into the natural rhythm of yourself, from where natural radiance and success stem.

Also, watch for overconfidence or self-important behaviour. Yes, you are thriving and succeeding, but do not become out of touch with yourself and others. It is important to be grounded, even when you are flying high.

XX ✦ JUDGEMENT

Use your judgement and higher power in service, not destruction

You are rising up, listening to your higher knowing and awakening to the power you hold within! You are letting go of burdens you have accumulated along your journey, including any anger or hurt you may hold others hostage to. Elevated and awakened, you are rising above your old self.

Judgement often appears when you are at a crossroads, needing to decide which direction to go or who to trust. You recognise you cannot choose based on your previous standards. Instead, you are reaching to make a decision from a higher perspective. It may feel as though you are being rebirthed and you are able to look back on who you were with fondness and love.

This is a card of illumination, understanding and light. Embrace your expansion. Give yourself space and time to understand the internal shifts you experience, and move into these changes so you may share who you are with others.

REVERSED

Stop for a moment, take a breath and *feel*. Do you need to realign? Are you placing too much emphasis on something or someone? Are you being critical of yourself or another? What is the internal discomfort you are feeling? Come back into your centre and power. You are generating a momentum of energy that is causing you dis-ease; now is the time to move back towards truth. This will be something you will feel, and it will feel good.

The reversed Judgement card may appear when you're faced with past actions. Perhaps you are considering a significant change, yet you feel contained by your past. Or perhaps another is holding you responsible for something from long ago. It is easy to choose a low energetic response. Instead, raise yourself higher!

XXI ✦ THE WORLD

Completion: the beginning and ending at once

A card of achievement and fulfilment, The World represents the completion of a cycle, bringing you full circle. You can now enjoy the experience of your dream brought to life. There is a deep feeling of contentment and success, perhaps even relief.

The World may also appear at the beginning of a journey. You are able to see the whole idea, knowing the adventure will take you to the depths and heights of who you are, leading you to where you envisage yourself. You embark, knowing that you are unfolding the mystery of the universe through your actions, and seeing the grander picture, where unity and wholeness are yours. This is clarity. Do not dismiss such clear knowing.

The World is a symbol of celebration and success. Mark your achievement! Share this triumph with others, or privately celebrate your hard work and expansion through ritual. It is important to lean into the delight of these moments before you hurry on to the next thing.

REVERSED

The quickest route to completion isn't always the most ideal. If you experience blocks in an endeavour, it may be because you are hurrying to the finish line without awareness of what this particular journey needs. You are overlooking important aspects that are vital for this venture's success. Stop, realign and reenergise by connecting to the initial vision before you continue forward.

Receiving this card reversed may also represent lack of closure. Perhaps something has ended suddenly and you have not yet reached a point of understanding or acceptance. Gently allow the wisdom of your inner being to guide you to a place of peace. Seeking answers from others can be helpful, but strength and knowing must ultimately come from within.

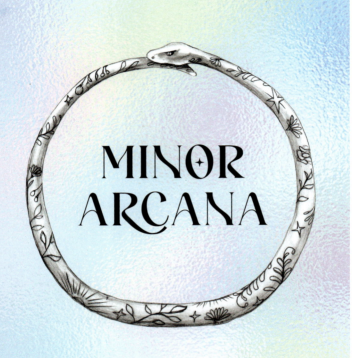

MINOR ARCANA

ACE of WANDS

Go for it!

The Ace of Wands is inspiration and action. This is a card of great creative power, signifying potency. Wands are fiery yang energy, evoking passion, will, vitality and momentum.

You are entering a significantly powerful phase of your life. A new relationship, creative endeavour, profession, study or business venture will consume your being, igniting you to step towards yourself and embrace the leader within. This is a time to listen to your instincts and potentially bend the rules a little. Trust that the inspired idea coupled with action will grow and develop, allowing you to use new game plans as this endeavour evolves. Take action *now*, rather than mull on it further. You are being supported by the stars and it is imperative you work with the energies at play.

The Ace of Wands can also signify a ground-breaking 'a-ha!' moment, allowing you to finally see a situation with clarity, especially if you have been lingering in the darkness, feeling uninspired and confused.

REVERSED

You may feel overwhelmed and confused, with too many competing ideas in your head to discern which is the most aligned decision. This lack of direction may leave you heavy and unmotivated, especially if there is pressure for you to participate in life in a certain way.

The reversed Ace of Wands may also come as an indicator that you are burdened and stifled by responsibility. Perhaps the potential for inspiration and action is there, but you are being blocked by a situation requiring your full attention and energy. This may be frustrating if you have grown past what is on offer currently.

Carve a little space for yourself. There is a path forward, it just requires you be committed to honouring yourself and the inspiration stirring within.

TWO OF WANDS

Step outside your comfort zone

This is the coupling of intuition and emotional intelligence with logical action and planning. You've taken a spark and run with it! Now you begin to actively weave it into life. You'll find yourself toggling between daydreaming and proactively ensuring this new venture gets off the ground.

You're in the process of reevaluating your responsibilities and rescheduling your days to ensure that time and focus are given to the goals you have set. You are feeling very aligned, connected and ready for this vibrant stage.

You are being called to step outside your comfort zone, think about your life and your desires in a new way and discover the potential and yearning within. You are ready to explore new worlds, so see this card as encouragement that you can make this happen!

Focus your energy, and move forward with confidence.

REVERSED

It is time to step boldly into what is calling you. Do your best to put aside the fear of the unknown, as it is causing you to feel diminished and depressed. Spend time tapping into the radiant potential and growth opportunity you have been presented, and see where it takes you. Start small and slowly if you need, but *start*. Revisit your own beliefs, values and goals, and be honest with yourself as to whether you are actually living these things.

This card may also indicate that you have an immediate need to reorganise and restructure elements of your life that have become unmanageable. This may be the result of taking on too much responsibility, some of which may be outside your scope of authority or knowledge.

There may also be a power struggle that requires addressing. Nip it in the bud, now.

THREE OF WANDS

THREE OF WANDS

Expanding your horizons

Any plan you have put into action has established a level of momentum and is calling for expansion. New opportunities lie ahead and you have the visionary insight to recognise them – even conjure them up! Use this time to connect with the people and institutions that will support you. Keep an open mind, as you may be called to consider options that lie outside of your initial ideas. Recognise that these potentialities will only add richness, should you decide to proceed.

Embrace the change that is afoot. Lift your eyes to the horizon and begin to look not only at your short-term but also your long-term goals. You are laying foundations that will see you succeed in the future. Now is the time for growth and expansion. Explore the great unknown, within yourself and within the opportunities around you. This is as much a journey of personal development as it is a life adventure.

The Three of Wands can also represent travel or the next phase of a relationship or business venture.

REVERSED

You may be experiencing a creative block, lack of momentum or growth, or disappointment of some kind. The more you look at this situation with a negative view, the more you will continue to feel frustrated. You need to realise that this is part of the journey and be truthful with yourself in regard to what may be holding you back.

There may have been a lack of foresight, causing you to deal with setbacks. This does not necessarily mean that the endeavour was misaligned, but take the time now to ensure that all elements of the process are taken care of.

In business, this card reversed may indicate a lack of communication between one or more parties, causing confusion and delay.

FOUR OF WANDS

Enjoying space and freedom

This is a card of celebration and freedom! You have committed to a vision and have reached a level of success, allowing you to sit back and enjoy the fruits of your hard work. While this is not the final stage in the venture, you have most certainly worked hard and reached the desired milestones. It is time now to let down your hair and rest. You have completed a significant phase in your life or project, so allow yourself to feel proud and be recognised for your efforts. Your visions and goals are being realised.

The Four of Wands is a time of harmony, joy and satisfaction in all areas of your life. You are feeling peaceful within yourself, and there is a deep and strong anchorage of energy within you, emanating out into your life.

Take this time to celebrate! Gather together with friends and family or simply give yourself time to breathe, relax and enjoy what you have achieved.

REVERSED

This card comes to you to provide courage and strength when it feels as though life's challenges are too daunting. Connect back to your motivation. Why did you embark down this path in the first place? What did you want to create and achieve? You are being reminded that often the most important and rewarding endeavours do not come easily, yet they will provide incredible satisfaction and joy when achieved.

You may potentially be going through a transition period, where you and your life seem unstable. Perhaps there is disharmony at home, at the workplace or within yourself. Turn your thoughts inner for solace and support. The answers you are seeking are held inside your very own lifeblood.

FIVE OF WANDS

Stand up for what you believe in

You are being called to stand up for your beliefs. This may be a time of struggle, competition or challenge, requiring you to stake your ground in a firm but kind and considerate manner. Keep an open mind and be in your own power should constructive criticism come your way, as it may be for your benefit and expansion.

The Five of Wands is a card of conflict. There is little ground being made due to conflicting ideas and visions, even if there is a common goal. It is wise to approach this time proactively and facilitate brainstorming sessions, open and transparent dialogue and problem-solving. Seek external mentoring with a knowledgeable counsel to ensure you are keeping a level head.

This card may also represent a personal problem that is causing tension. Perhaps you feel conflicted as to how you're going to navigate forward while external forces oppose your ideals. Go with what feels most right and aligned for you.

REVERSED

Are you running away from conflict or not wanting to recognise your role within a situation? How are you going to grow and learn if you continue to avoid uncomfortable situations? By avoiding conflict, you are squashing an opportunity to raise your own concerns. Start by gathering your thoughts and centring your energy. Then approach the situation intending to resolve the issues.

On the opposite spectrum, this may mark a breakthrough and relief! Finally, an outcome has been negotiated and you are feeling at ease and satisfied. This can include relationship and internal conflict. You have worked through any anger, resentment or grievances that may have been holding you or the relationship back, allowing you now to move forward.

SIX OF WANDS

Riding out the storm to success

You have managed to negotiate any confusion and setbacks, seeing you now a little wiser and somewhat transformed. By embracing your natural skills and strengths and focusing this energy into one goal, you are nearing the finish line, which will see you stand out from the crowd and come out on top!

For some time now you have been working hard at creating an authentic life, inside and out, building reputation and respect within your community for how you conduct yourself and what you do. You may be increasingly recognised for your personal ethics, unique style and natural talent. Now is not the time to be shy – let yourself and all you've worked hard for shine!

Appreciate your own worth and allow others to do so. You are inspiring and are living the life of example. Good work.

REVERSED

You are misaligned in your thoughts and energy. Maybe you are feeling less-than, or lacking the self-belief, strength and confidence to forge forward. This may come from spending too much time comparing yourself to others, which denies and erodes your own skills and gifts. Pay more attention to your thoughts and course-correct them when you notice you are indulging in comparison and self-criticism.

This card may also be suggesting that you are trying to achieve too many things at once, leaving you flustered, unfocused and dissatisfied with your lot in life. Strip your endeavours, goals and commitments back to only what is necessary and important. Connect with who you are, not who you believe you need to be.

SEVEN OF WANDS

Back yourself and be the light

You may be being called to back yourself and trust your own inner source of light. Your passion and resolve are being tested and, despite feeling uncertain, you welcome the occasion! You can feel the energy and vitality of what you stand for burning within you. You are being called to stand tall, to light the way for others.

Trust in yourself and your vision. Be the representative who speaks with power and heart so that others may hear you. Know that you are right to believe in yourself and what you stand for. Discard any fear or uncertainty at this time – you and all you've created are too aligned not to flourish.

REVERSED

Perhaps you are feeling continually judged, criticised and questioned by those around you. This may be undermining your self-esteem and self-belief, causing you to flounder and feel confused and angry. Trust that only you can see what it is you are working towards, and that in time, should you continue to commit to what your soul is asking of you, others will understand and see it too. Until then, stay strong and pull back on sharing too much information too soon.

EIGHT OF WANDS

Up and flying! Your second wind

The Eight of Wands strikes at your heart like a lighting bolt of clarity and alignment. You have been seeking this kind of electricity in your life for some time, and are now rising out of the somewhat sticky slump you were in to feel the vitality of opportunity return.

By harnessing this energy, you are able to build increased momentum towards the goals and activities you wish to see into their fullness, at a pace you haven't been able to achieve before. This is your second wind, allowing you to put strategies and plans in place with ease and grace, creating progress. Right now you're filled with passion, focus and optimism for the future. Do all you can to support these wonderful vibrations so that you may succeed.

Be mindful that you do not rush for the sake of hurrying along completion. While you have wonderful energy and momentum behind you, it is important that you use your intuitive wisdom and logic to make smart decisions and actions.

REVERSED

While you may be filled with enthusiasm for your returned inspiration and energy, you may be finding that you're conflicted by so many worthy ideas, leaving you confused and frustrated. It is important to understand that, while all of the inspired ideas are valuable, it is important to hone your focus towards the most aligned avenue of action so that you complete your vision and the cycle of creation.

This card reversed may also symbolise potential delays and setbacks in regard to important activities, goals or actions. While frustrating, use the setback wisely. Do not allow it to undo all your hard work, emotionally or energetically. You may also need to seek alternatives.

NINE OF WANDS

The end is in sight

You may feel worn out and as though it is hard to go on, but you don't have far to go now. Fear and uncertainty may rise up, but know that this is normal and natural when nearing completion. Courage and resilience are needed. Draw on all you have achieved and feel secure in the stability you have created. This is an internal test – do your best not to waver.

The Nine of Wands can represent one final setback or inconvenience. While it may be wise to consider the worst scenario, do not give it your energy. View it as an opportunity to practise diligence.

Along this internal or material journey, you may have experienced loss and setbacks, potentially leaving you distrustful of others. Acknowledge all that you have learned and gained, and release whatever is unnecessary.

REVERSED

Have the boundaries and goals you have set for yourself become your cage? Have you been feeling tense or uptight? This card may be a reminder that, while your boundaries, structures and focus have supported you, they may be causing you to feel irritated and somewhat trapped. Also be mindful of any judgement towards yourself or others. You may like to spice things up by easing back on routines and expectations. Now would be a wonderful time for self-care: indulge in a mini getaway or stay-in retreat.

This card may prompt you to reconsider your outlook towards an aspiration. You may have been feeling the burden of responsibility due to the size and involvement of the task, yet you are being encouraged to also look at the reward and satisfaction it would give you. Do not forget that life is as much about personal growth and aligned challenges as it is about fun.

TEN of WANDS

Accept the support of others

A card of completion and responsibility. You have worked hard for all you have achieved, and while you may feel satisfied with the fruits of your efforts, you are beginning to understand the responsibility that comes with them. Having completed a major goal, you can feel inspired and excited, and at the same time burdened by what ongoing commitment may entail.

We fill our plates to the brim, generous in our time and ambitious in our goals. This card may highlight that now is the time to seek the support of others to alleviate some tasks.

Assess what is required of you personally and delegate what can be shared with others.

The Ten of Wands may also highlight that you are feeling undervalued and overused within a current situation, seeing you carrying the brunt of the load. It is time to rectify this situation and to put measures in place for rest.

REVERSED

You may have come to the realisation that you are unnecessarily holding on to duties and responsibilities, and worrying about matters that are either out of your control or none of your concern. Get clear on what is causing undue pressure, and either let go of those tasks, readjust your perspective or seek the support of others.

This card reversed may appear to let you know that challenging times are nearly over. You may feel as though it's been one challenge after the next and you are ready for a reprieve. Take a sigh of relief, as it won't be long until you are more at ease in all areas of your life.

Be realistic about your needs and capacity from now and into the future. You are of no use when you are strung out and exhausted.

MAIDEN OF WANDS

MAIDEN OF WANDS

Wild and free

Change is in the air! Feel the fiery spark of enthusiasm, driving you to break free from anything that has you feeling trapped. You may begin to push the parameters of your life, sensing that a new adventure awaits. Be both bold and grounded enough to step into this dynamic energy that your soul is ready to explore.

You may feel a defining moment nearing. You are being encouraged to connect with and express your own sense of self, tapping into your pure truth as the light to guide you forward. This card may come at a time when you are seeking freedom, perhaps even tasting the kind of unbridled freedom that ignites you with abundant energy. Express your playfulness! It is time to set aside all the rules you have adhered to and truly turn up for yourself in a transformative way.

The Maiden of Wands has a passion for life and an unquenchable thirst for movement and action, always seeking new horizons and being a catalyst for change. She is a straight-talking, genuine woman who thinks outside the square and doesn't like to be put in a box. With diverse skills and a wonderful intellect, she is a valued member of any project and a welcome sight at any gathering.

REVERSED

Are you experiencing a negative response from others when you share your enthusiasm, leaving you uncertain and disgruntled? Understand that this is to be expected when forging your own path or instigating change. Alternatively, you may have initiated action, only to be blocked by external factors or complexities, leaving you unmotivated and lacking direction.

The Maiden of Wands can be a flighty or erratic individual, lacking self-belief. They may feel insecure, leading them to partake in gossiping, petty quarrelling or pessimism.

KNIGHT of WANDS

KNIGHT of WANDS

Galloping in pursuit!

You are feeling confident and connected. There has been significant action and your commitment to bravely moving forward is visible to those around you. You may feel swept up in all you've undertaken, your energy swinging from vital to flat, but you're managing yourself well. Keep a level head and move forward methodically, even when you want to rush ahead.

The Knight of Wands is a great communicator who easily elicits support and backing from those around him. He is sociable and charming, with the desire to live to the full.

He can be opinionated and rigid in his view, and is known to act without thinking. Despite his warm exterior, the Knight of Wands can be hard to know. He takes pride in his work and bringing ideas to life. He enjoys the satisfaction at the end of an endeavour, only to quickly pursue another adventure.

You are on the right track. Act on any hunches or opportunities presented.

REVERSED

You're exhausted and near burnout. You have been going full throttle, with little time to refuel. You may be feeling frustrated and without energy to carry on. If you are considering walking away from a venture, take time to regroup first. Rash decisions may leave you regretful.

The Knight of Wands can be a sign of impulsive action brought on by the desire to fix everything at once. Some things cannot be hurried; part of the journey is allowing things to have their own process rather than always pushing forward.

The Knight of Wands can be an individual who steamrolls others, unaware or uncaring of how their behaviour affects those around them. They may be erratic in thought and action, leaving ruin and rubble behind them; all bravado, yet scared and alone internally.

QUEEN OF WANDS

QUEEN OF WANDS

Limitless potential

The natural and radiant leader within you is seeking to emerge. There are passions near your heart that you are being called to put into action. Recognise your limitless potential: you are capable of achieving whatever you desire. Align yourself with your vision, focus your mindset and stride forward! The example you lead with will create curiosity among those around you. Through your actions, you encourage others to consider what they are being internally guided towards.

Your vision, determination and positivity, even when challenges arise, make others seek you out when in need of support. You mix realism and optimism, instilling confidence in others, which builds your own self-belief.

The Queen of Wands may be a strong, vibrant 'mover and shaker' in your life, or this card may be calling you to recognise the Wand Queen within. She is not afraid to go out on a limb when passionate: an independent woman living by her own rules, successfully creating a life of abundance and success.

REVERSED

Have you recently lost confidence, leaving you angry, frustrated and even aggressive towards others? While you may have experienced setbacks, it is important that you come to see them as opportunities and not lean towards victimhood. Focus on balancing yourself through activities that fill you up and reconnect you with your sense of self.

This card may also warn of someone resentful and jealous, acting in a bullying manner.

The Queen of Wands can be determined to the point of being rigid and stubborn, causing inflexibility in her external world and within herself. She is fiery by nature, which often serves her well but at times causes difficulty and heartache. A complicated woman, she's a powerful force to be reckoned with when her energies are channelled in the right direction.

KING OF WANDS

Motivational and innovative

You have the ability to be a very strong leader, able to see a clear potential future and willing to put in the hard yards and do the work. Your journey thus far has led you to a place where you are no longer investing yourself in people or ventures you don't deem worthwhile. You are naturally compassionate and ensure others feel valued. You navigate calmly through complex situations and can think outside the box.

The King of Wands is pure fire energy. Years of self-exploration have enabled the Wand King to know himself and refine his creation process. His creativity lies in dynamically seeing a venture through – especially one that has the power to affect many people. A natural-born entrepreneur, he articulates his vision so potently that he easily enlists the support of others. An adrenaline junkie, the King of Wands enjoys taking calculated risks to bring something to life or resolve a challenge. It is part of what makes him a game changer.

This card may encourage you to cultivate some of these latent qualities inside yourself to bring an idea to fruition. It may also indicate that you should seek the wise counsel of a mentor or guide to support you through this phase of your life.

REVERSED

Are your expectations for yourself or others too high? While it is important to have a full vision, it takes baby steps to get there. Stop moving the goal posts, and celebrate small victories. Are you placing too much emphasis on external validation to drive and inspire you forward? Just because people may not understand doesn't mean you shouldn't forge forward.

ACE of CUPS

The joy of blossoming

The Ace of Cups indicates the stirring of your inner spring of love, joy, emotion, creativity and optimism. You are entering a new phase, potentially seeing you enter into a romantic relationship, friendship or divinely aligned business partnership, leading to further growth and opportunity.

The Ace of Cups may also represent a time of self-care and self-exploration. Perhaps you have been feeling exciting yet unfamiliar energy within you, calling you to explore different areas of interest and aspects of yourself. This will feel exciting, adventurous and at times nerve-racking as you step further into the soul-guided elements of yourself that are ready for expression.

A card of celebration, fertility, birth, renewal and making a new start! It is a joyous time, where good health, aligned choices and connected friendships are able to develop and thrive.

Give yourself permission to follow your intuition and gut. Let yourself quiet the noise in your mind.

REVERSED

Sadness, disconnection and a feeling of loss may be present. This card may herald an ending of a relationship, friendship or way you relate to another person, denoting that your soul contract has been completed. This card may also be the ending and accompanying mourning of an aspect of yourself.

You must embrace yourself and your life with fullness and love, for you are responsible for your own happiness. Life is full of contrast, which is vital for growth. It is what you do with this contrast that is most important. What can you do to realign yourself?

What lies behind another's intentions? Observe the guidance of your body. What is it telling you? Perhaps now is not the most appropriate time to move ahead with an endeavour or relationship, intimate or otherwise. Trust your instincts.

TWO of CUPS

Connection and balance, yin and yang

The Two of Cups is the archetype of balance and harmony. There is a natural ebb and flow, give-and-take synergy between oneself and another – be that an intimate relationship, or financial or professional harmony – ensuring there is balance within oneself and one's life.

Traditionally, the Two of Cups is associated with twin-soul love, where connection is pure, honest, solid and respectful. If there are challenges within a relationship, look deeper than the surface level for reharmonisation.

This is a card of love: budding relationships and developing a connection that rejuvenates the soul and flows into all areas of one's life. It may also indicate that a quarrel or mistake can be mended and healed.

If you are ready to call more love into your life, take this as a sign that the universe has heard your desires.

REVERSED

This card speaks of conflict and problems within a relationship. Perhaps the natural flow, cooperation and consideration is not present, or a level of dishonesty has found its way between your connection. Something has shifted in your dynamic, potentially stemming from a personal, internal shift within yourself or the other person involved. A new platform of communion will need to be cultivated for the relationship to thrive, as your current way of relating to each other is no longer working.

Individually, the Two of Cups may bring the message that you are at a crossroads within yourself, leaving you feeling depressed, confused or internally conflicted. Instead of attempting to run away from the discomfort of this feeling, it is time to explore it, making more of a commitment to yourself, your passions and your natural gifts.

THREE OF CUPS

Expansion, connection and celebration

A time of celebration and success shared with friends and family. You have stretched past your comfort zone and created abundance and beauty in your life that you are now able to share. This is a time to reflect upon all your growth and effort, enjoying the excitement and possibilities of the future with those special kindred people close to you.

Freely and openly offer your skills, presence and positive outlook to others, and receive what they have to offer in return. There is a sense of community, connection, understanding and aligned consciousness.

This card may also symbolise the conception or birth of something, whether a pregnancy or the creative spark leading you to participate in a group setting of like minds with a common goal or agenda.

There is playful and vibrant energy around you.

REVERSED

Are you stifling your divine inspiration and soul's desire? This card comes as a gentle encouragement to acknowledge what your core essence is trying to express, so you feel uplifted and fulfilled. This *will* happen, and you will also open yourself up to a community of people who encourage and support you in your endeavours.

This card may also indicate social isolation. Maybe you have been so consumed in your work that you have let go of friendships and social activity. This may have been needed initially, but take this reversed card as a sign to rekindle your friendships, as they offer you support and respite, refilling and recharging you. On the flip side, you may have been overindulging in social activity to the detriment of other aspects of your life.

Within relationships, this card may highlight instability, unhappiness or tension. Past experiences may require important conversations and a reestablishment of boundaries and values.

FOUR OF CUPS

The power is in your hands

From the outside looking in, the world would see you and your life as somewhat perfect – full of pleasure, success and fulfilment in all areas, maybe even excessively so. And yet, within your skin and bones you feel a deep discontent. Perhaps you have worked hard, only to feel entrapped by your creations. Or maybe you are regretting not taking another path. Now is the time to dive deep within your inner world to understand your desires, so you can make powerful choices about your life.

The Four of Cups comes as a message that decisions are to be made; as the designer and creator of your life, they are to be made by you only. Create space to take stock. Ensure that you are not taking your life for granted, for this card may show that you have become hollow in your hunger for happiness, which only ever results in ingratitude and disappointment.

The power is in your hands. Fill yourself up spiritually, open your eyes and really see the bounty that surrounds you. Decide what it is you are truly desiring and step towards it.

REVERSED

You are breaking free of a situation where you have felt trapped and stagnant. You have recognised that your heart and soul yearned for more, and you went for it! This takes courage and determination.

You have put in the inner work and matched it with external action; you're now seeing shifts and movement in your life, letting you know that things are indeed changing. Focus on any final steps to make the transition from where you have been to where you are wanting to be.

Let down any barriers that hold you back from speaking your truth and sharing your heart.

FIVE OF CUPS

Healing or self-destruction

Not all has gone to plan. Recently you may have experienced some kind of loss: the ending of a relationship, the loss of a position or job, the loss of a loved one, or a betrayal. You are now deep in the grief and challenge of this setback.

The Five of Cups suggests that you are having difficulty accepting and letting go. Instead of moving forward, you are choosing to stay in a place of lack. Happiness and opportunities are being missed because you are dwelling on the past.

Self-pity and blame need to stop. It is time to heal. Begin to practise forgiveness and acceptance. Understand that there are some things out of your control, and move with them. Embrace what you *can* do and lift your eyes to the horizon, for there is light at the end of the tunnel.

REVERSED

This is a friendly and playful reminder to stop beating yourself up! It is okay to be sad, but do not let this stop you in your tracks. Give yourself space to grieve, but ensure that it is in a cathartic, not self-destructive, way. Playing the victim will get you nowhere. This card reversed may also indicate that an old wound has resurfaced for you to finally work through. See this as an opportunity, rather than getting stuck in the murky rut of the past.

There is immense value in this pain, and you are beginning to recognise the beauty and power in the lessons it has offered you. Perhaps you feel encouraged to take a risk – a bold step forward, filled with hope for the future. You are increasingly aligned to yourself and your desires. Rather than feeling trapped by the past, you are beginning to feel empowered by the wisdom gained.

SIX OF CUPS

The sweet scent of memories

The Six of Cups represents nostalgia and happiness. Take a walk down memory lane, on your own or perhaps with an old friend from the past. Sinking into uplifting memories – times you felt connected and free – can be a wonderful navigational tool as you create.

There is an element of balance to be heeded with this card. It is useful and healthy to reflect on the past, especially when reconnecting with aspects of yourself that you wish to cultivate again. Yet take care not to become so attached to the past that you forget to enjoy life.

This is a beautiful card, denoting a carefree freshness. It may indicate that you will soon return to a familiar stomping ground. Enjoy the lightness and joy of this time, let your inner child come out to play and squirrel away the gifts the past is offering you.

REVERSED

Being in the present is the message here. You are spending too much time living in the past or thinking about the future. Very little of your self is in the now.

There may be issues from your past that you are required to make peace with and heal. They are resurfacing now because they play an integral role in the choices and decisions you must make for the future. Seek support from friends, family, energy workers or specialists if you need assistance in understanding them and moving forward.

This card may be a gentle reminder that creating presence is the key to finding what you are searching for. The past can never be recreated, and the future is based on what you are projecting now. So what are you projecting?

Call all elements of yourself back in and allow yourself to be radiant and whole.

SEVEN OF CUPS

From daydreams to living the dream

Beautiful daydreams that are soul inspired and live only in your head and heart are ready and calling for you to bring them into life. You are powerfully creative, with wonderful ideas that need to be shared with the world. This requires action, strategy and focus. Your dreams can be made a reality should you accept the challenge and adventure they are offering. Expand outside your comfort zone and come to know yourself as the visionary and alchemist you are.

Do not allow yourself to be consumed by the fear of stepping into the unknown. Be clear in your heart and mind as to what you desire to create and why, and then stick close to this, as it will be the fuel that will sustain you through any tribulations.

Be wise with your decisions. Do not allow illusions and unrealistic ideals to prevent sound choices. Allow yourself to dream big, yet understand that to reach those dreams you must create strong foundations and consistently take small steps towards them.

REVERSED

This card comes as a warning, indicating that you are being tempted by illusions of grandeur and unrealistic fantasies. Perhaps you have your head in the clouds, unwilling to deal with day-to-day realities.

You may be unclear about what you desire, or fearful about stepping into yourself, taking a risk and putting your dreams and desires on the line.

Take time to go inwards and face off the resistance. Explore why you are more comfortable living in the dreams and illusions of your head. You will begin to see clearly as soon as you accept that you are yearning for more of who you really are, and that you are responsible for holding yourself back.

EIGHT OF CUPS

EIGHT OF CUPS

Transition and change, a spiritual journey

You feel the internal stirrings of a metaphorical death or ending, calling you deeply within and revealing that it is time to walk away from parts of your life that you have created and step into the darkness of no-thing. You may be exhausted from pursuing a life that is only skin deep.

This may be acknowledgment that a venture did not work out as you imagined it would. Or it may be that your initial vision, having come to fruition, did not bring the deep internal connection you were seeking. You are ready to walk away from your former creations in search of truth and meaning. You may have concluded that the material life and the steps that society expects you to follow are not what your soul yearns for.

This may be a time of disappointment, loss and confusion, but trust in the knowledge that by turning away from what is familiar yet unfulfilling, you are embarking on a journey of self-discovery.

REVERSED

This may indicate that you are at a crossroad, faced with a significant choice, yet feeling confused as to which path to take. While you are not ready to move on, it is clear that you are dissatisfied with your current situation.

You may need to let go of relationships or situations, leaving them unresolved and trusting that the future will bring completion. Truthfulness and transparency are needed, even within yourself, so that you can move out of this current state.

Purge your life of all that is unnecessary, so you have space to move and breathe again. Accept that your beliefs and values may have changed and that this is needed for transformation. From darkness springs growth. Trust in the process and have confidence in yourself.

NINE OF CUPS

The fruits of alignment

A sign of harmony, abundance and satisfaction – you are now experiencing the emotional and material reward of going within and aligning yourself and your life. The Nine of Cups reflects happiness and dreams come true. Your fears regarding whether you would succeed in creating a life that reflects your soul have now disappeared. You've done it! You are now spurred on to continue creating with vitality and light.

Count your blessings, acknowledging the hard work you have put in – spiritually and physically – growing your life to this point. Take a breath and enjoy the deep sense of contentment. Your foundations are solid and your worries are in the past.

This is an emotionally fulfilling time. Relationships may be blooming, friendships and business opportunities are solidifying and your finances are on the up. You have paved your way to success, and it's now about sharing and celebrating with others, enjoying life's pleasures. You have healed the past and are ready to create more of what your heart desires.

REVERSED

Your dreams and desires will not materialise through little effort. Manifestation requires visioning, inner work and strategy. Frustration or disappointment at the minimal reward you have received may be due to lack of commitment and action. Preconceived expectations of what you should have achieved by now may have been unrealistic.

There may be the sense of emptiness or of something missing. Listen and learn from this feeling: it is trying to guide you into alignment. Perhaps you have not properly addressed your fears around being authentically yourself, and so continue to operate just on the surface.

Do you want to know yourself? Are you willing to reveal who you are to the world? Your level of success is dependent on your willingness to be real.

TEN OF CUPS

Magnetic fulfilment, abounding love

Stop for a moment and take a breath. You have reached the place you envisaged. Your life is overflowing with love in its many shades. You have followed your heart, trusted your intuition and clarified your values, putting them all into action. Only success and fulfilment can follow.

You are radiating beautiful vibrations of gratitude and joy for the prosperity and abundance in your life, and you willingly share what you have with others. Close friends, family and the surrounding community feel safe within your arms, and the love you give is returned twofold. You are a guiding light and an inspiration for what it is to step into your power and truth and become who you know you are.

REVERSED

Are your beliefs and values aligned with the actions and choices you are making? Are you pursuing material goals at the expense of your relationships? And are the material goals you are pursuing a true reflection of what your heart really desires?

This card reversed comes as a warning that, should you not address your current lifestyle and behaviours, you may find that your relationships and family life could be greatly compromised. While your intentions may be pure, your choices are coming at the expense of your personal values, while eroding the love and connection that supports you in life.

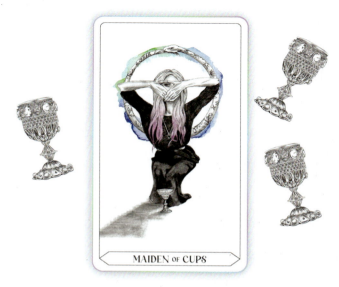

MAIDEN OF CUPS

Dare to dream, follow your intuitive leads

Your creative, free, vibrant and intuitive inner child is inspiring your imagination. You are opening to possibilities that you may have believed were not viable to you. This is a card of encouragement and new beginnings. Pay attention to this fresh energy your subconscious is delivering, as you are being guided and are supported by the universe to birth this magical creation.

It is important to feel connected and confident in the information your higher self is gifting you before you share it with others, as there is the risk that they will try to deter you, leaving you deflated and untrusting.

The Maiden of Cups may appear as a vibrant, whimsical woman in your life, or may reflect elements of yourself. Her head is often in the clouds and her heart is full of dreams and aspirations. She is a sensitive, intuitive and creative creature who may flit from one thing to the next due to being ungrounded or feeling unworthy.

Follow the guided inspiration you're receiving and explore your intuitive and creative process.

REVERSED

A gentle reminder that you are not your emotions. It is imperative that you control your tendency to indulge in drama and emotional turmoil, as it will only lead to self-destruction. Recognise that you are an intuitive and sensitive being who easily picks up the energy and emotions of others. Discern what is yours and what is another's baggage. It is time for you to stop childish and immature behaviours and step into your power as a gifted creator.

The reversed Maiden of Cups may also indicate a creative block or lack of inspiration. It is time to rest and rejuvenate, allowing the creative juices to flow once more. Be mindful that not all dreams are realistic. Ensure that you are balancing your aspirations with common sense.

KNIGHT OF CUPS

Be bold in your love

It is a time of creative action and passion. You are being called to start something that ignites your heart and soul. This may be a new activity, hobby, business or relationship, or enrolling in a course that sets you alight! There is no need to rush with this new venture: it is important that the foundations be built out of love, your inner strength and creativity, to ensure that you continue to stay invested and inspired.

This card may come as a nudge forward, encouraging you to turn that hobby or interest into a living or to potentially have a friendship move into a relationship. Be open to the guidance of your heart.

The Knight of Cups may also be a person who demonstrates unwavering passion and charm, using these traits to his advantage in the pursuit of relationships and the acceptance of others. He is ruled more by his heart than his head, which can lead to him being taken advantage of. It may also mean that he is unable to truly commit to any one person or thing, as he is enticed by every shiny object or person that catches his heart and eye.

REVERSED

Perhaps a seemingly appealing situation or person has turned out to be no more than empty promises, leaving you disappointed and feeling betrayed. Upon reflection you realise you were wearing rose-coloured glasses, believing that something external to yourself would bring you the joy and love your heart is craving. Do not wallow in self-pity and blame – see this for what it is: a lesson that you are the only one who can bring yourself happiness.

Do not become entangled in overly emotional states of jealousy or depression. You do not want to spend your life swinging from one extreme to another.

QUEEN of CUPS

QUEEN of CUPS

Nurturing all aspects of your life successfully

You have harnessed the gifts of your intuition and emotions to create a life where you are the expression of your heart's desires, understanding that being grounded and stable is vital for the creation of your desires.

You have high understanding and empathy, often counselling others and supporting them to find themselves and navigate forward, aligned with who they are. You trust in the universe and your communion with it, knowing that a part of your purpose here is to support and guide others in developing this connection for themselves. You often act as a beacon of light and an example of what it is to embody sensitivity *and* strength.

This card may also come as a prompt to recognise these attributes and traits within yourself and actively cultivate their presence in your daily life. You may find that there is a strong, calm and intuitive person you can rely on to mentor you through a process or undertaking.

REVERSED

Are you allowing your imagination or emotions to run away with you? Or perhaps it is the opposite: are you feeling repressed and deeply out of touch with your intuition and inner self? This card is calling you to return to your centre. You are a wise and powerful individual who is deeply connected to the language of the universe. It is time for you to embrace your knowledge, stepping into your power as a leader and beacon of radiance and light.

Rid yourself of low-vibrating, self-destructive behaviours. On occasion these methods have worked for you, yet your soul knows that choosing to respond and interact with life in this way leaves you heavy, as you carry around the energetic incongruences of your choices.

KING OF CUPS

Master of your inner and outer worlds

Your emotional maturity, intuitive intelligence and calm stability are to be capitalised upon or cultivated. The King of Cups represents the balance between the head and the heart, and the seen and unseen worlds. You have the ability to balance emotional and creative inspiration with logic and strategy. This enables you to be a true leader, creating and recognising opportunity, as well as seeing the spiritual lesson within every challenge. If you are being called to step up and lead, take this as your sign.

You may recognise the qualities of the King of Cups within yourself, or in a male mentor figure within your life and community. Strengths such as empathy, compassion and keen listening skills, coupled with emotional intelligence, business acumen and wisdom gathered, may be what you are being encouraged to harness.

The King of Cups can also be a very auspicious sign of a potential charming and charismatic mate, representative of lasting love and fidelity should you be opening yourself to love.

REVERSED

Are you riddled with insecurities? Are you managing them through controlling and manipulative behaviours or emotional outbursts? Or perhaps you depend too much on external validation and direction, clouding your decision making as you are always viewing yourself through the eyes of what others will think. This indicates that you are not standing in your own power. See this card as a message for you to begin the journey into your own inner strength, so you and others can come to know you as the leader you are.

It may also be that you are experiencing a crisis of the heart, feeling torn between two possible pathways or options.

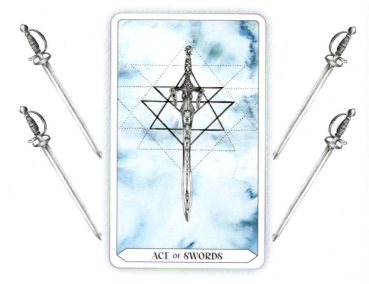

ACE OF SWORDS

Potent power, clear thinking, spiritual insight

There is not a lot that can stop you right now! The power that lies behind you is potent. The Ace of Swords has gifted you the insight you have been seeking for some time regarding a situation or issue at hand, leading you to reach such dynamic clarity of thought that all other distractions or complexities fall away. However, it is somewhat of a double-edged sword, as the more you push for truth the further away you get from it. Relax. Take the path of least resistance.

This is a period full of original thought, calling for you to seize opportunities as they surface. If you are emerging from a difficult period, this is a wonderful card to receive: the fog is lifting and you are returning to your centre, recalibrated and ready. It is wise for you to use the lessons you have learned in a beneficial way, for the greater good of yourself and those around you. You may be ready to pursue new opportunities, such as learning a new skill or further study.

Decisions are to be made and actions are to be taken. Your consciousness is reaching expanded levels of awareness and spiritual connection. Use this to your advantage.

REVERSED

You are not seeing a situation from its fullest perspective. It is time to take a step back for clarity to be reached, as things have digressed to a state where continuing to push forward will be futile.

This card may also represent that you have disconnected from your own internal source of power and wisdom. You are being urged to come back to your centre, to stop running from the truth in your heart. Believe in your own power and spiritual source.

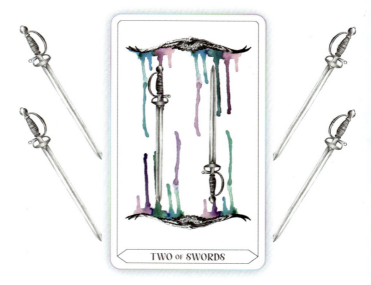

TWO OF SWORDS

Decisions to make

This is the card of choice: there are decisions to be made and you may be feeling torn as to which direction to take. Avoiding the situation only creates more fear and congestion of energy, stagnating your internal waters and causing undue fog and confusion. Running away from making a choice has you sitting outside your personal power and it is time to step up and make the best decision for yourself and where you are at right now.

This card may also indicate that you are at a stalemate. Abandoning the situation does not mean it will go away. Know that there will be no good nor bad outcome from your decision, simply movement. This is what is needed to see energy expand once more, allowing for new opportunities.

Make peace with yourself, any others involved and the situation as a whole. Come back into your own power – balance will be restored through participation. Trust in the greater good.

Alternatively, you may be able to clearly cut through any confusion with ease. This may not mean others will agree with your decision; however, no harm will come.

REVERSED

Mental confusion and information overload is rife! You are not only feeling frustrated by the opposing options, but also by the input of others and their energy. Know that not all of what you are feeling is yours – you are also carrying residual energy of those around you. Take time to yourself. Listen to your internal guidance and go from there. Do so quietly if need be, so as not to be influenced by others.

You may also find you're in the middle of another's conflict. Is this really your role to play, or are you complicating matters further?

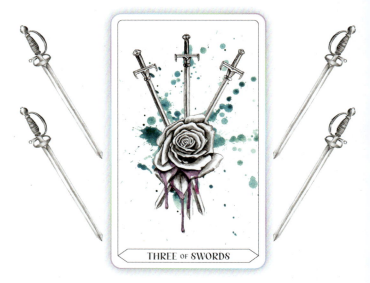

THREE of SWORDS

THREE OF SWORDS

Sadness, pain, sacrifice

A card of disappointment and pain. An outcome or relationship may not go as you desired. There is no point in resisting or avoiding the inevitable truth. Sadness is a natural part of growth; while walking through a time of discomfort or rejection, know that you will come through the other side stronger. Pain lets us move towards its opposing energy: joy. Be gentle on yourself. Practise self-care and know that you will come to view this situation as an opportunity for growth.

This card may also represent the need to release something you have been carrying, whether material, situational or emotional. You have been holding on to something that is inhibiting your potential and it is time to let go. Express how you are feeling, seek the support of others if needed, and create a release ritual. Honour yourself. While this may feel like walking into the unknown, you are ready for what lies on the other side.

REVERSED

The silver lining to a dark cloud. Potentially you have just come through a difficult time of loss. While you may still be feeling raw, you see the light at the end of the tunnel. Be mindful that you are not holding yourself back from healing. Becoming too comfortable with sadness only leads to inner disconnection. Be guided by your internal energy – if it is encouraging you to walk forward and put yourself out there again, follow this lead.

This card may denote that you are finding it challenging to move past the pain you have experienced. Perhaps this is because you are not willing to go to the root cause of the sadness, or you do not feel safe and supported to work through it. It is now time to forgive and let go of the emotions and stories that anchor you to the past.

FOUR OF SWORDS

Rest, reevaluation, realignment

The Four of Swords is urging you to rest and rejuvenate. Yet this is not a passive process! You must understand what restores you and actively carve out time to engage in these realigning and revitalising activities. This may also mean that an integration of shadow aspects of yourself is needed. By doing this, you will expand not only your depth of knowledge but also your conscious awareness and intuitive abilities.

This is a time of identifying what fills you up and what depletes you. Each time you step towards more of the people and activities you enjoy, you step towards more of yourself, restoring faith, self-belief and life energy. Do your best to pinch off spiralling thoughts of stress and overwhelm, realigning yourself back to your centre and to what you recognise as your own truth.

If you recently reached and completed a milestone, it is vital for you to take time to enjoy the aftermath of its success and completion. Do not rush forward immediately. Create space so you may get to know this new you.

REVERSED

You may be feeling opposing forces within you. Your body and emotions may be frayed and calling for time out, yet your mind is racing. You may be having difficulty sleeping or settling yourself enough to be able to rest and recoup on a daily basis. If this is the case, it is vital for you to take appropriate measures.

This card reversed can also imply that you may be frustrated with a lack of progress and the natural evolution of your life and intimate relationships. You may feel empty or stagnant. Yet this has a lot to do with your unwillingness to address what needs to be addressed and be more active in the process of growth.

FIVE OF SWORDS

Winner or loser

A card of disillusionment and mistrust. There is conflict: maybe a situational struggle, or emotional or mental discord. You may find yourself disagreeing with others, feeling tension and generally being hostile towards the world. This may stem from patterns of low thought or due to others losing faith in you. While your ambitious nature may have achieved what you wanted, it has potentially come at the expense of others. This will never feel like a win and you are now dealing with the aftermath. Take a step back and reconnect with your core values. What is really important to you? Are you willing to alienate yourself and hurt others for the sake of winning? The Five of Swords may also mean that a trusted person is undermining or betraying you.

This card can simply mean defeat – you have given your best efforts and not succeeded. Winning does not always mean success. You may not have achieved what you set out to achieve, but this doesn't mean you haven't grown or had other successes. Do not discard or undervalue what you have learned through the process.

REVERSED

A reversed Five of Swords represents change after a period of conflict. You are willing to lay down your sword and openly begin to negotiate a path forward, having taken time to reflect and look at the situation with fresh eyes. You are ready for balance and harmony to return to your life, making now a good time to reach out to other parties who may be involved in resolving tension.

If the dis-ease and conflict has been internal, due to a past wound or trauma, this card is letting you know that it is time to safely revisit and resolve it. Allow the universe and your inner knowing to support you, guiding you forward with love.

SIX OF SWORDS

Recovery from difficult times

After a period of uncertainty and unrest, you are headed towards happier days. You may be feeling heavy, depressed and like you're in the thick of a transition period, but keep working through it. Let go and surrender what is no longer serving you, and listen to the guidance within. Take this opportunity to reassess your beliefs and values slowly, exploring the depth and breadth of your beauty and your evolving internal worlds. You are moving away from your past and who you used to be, and towards who you are becoming.

This is a time of learning and growth. Clarity and more prosperous times lie ahead, so it's important you begin to chart a path forward, reflective of your heart. Back your intuition and combine it with logic so you may sail towards the stars. Trust and know that there is fun and hope for the future.

It is a time to make decisions for yourself.

REVERSED

You may be doubting the decisions you have made because of challenges that have arisen or slow movement that isn't reflective of your effort. This may be due to unresolved past issues or attachments. It may be helpful to look under the surface of your life, rather than attempting to run away from or ignore it. A reversed Six of Swords, from a relationship perspective, may also mean you haven't moved on from a past love.

This card can also represent that you are resentful and unwilling to move forward, due to feeling as though you weren't included in a decision that was potentially out of your hands. It is time to embrace and enjoy the changes that are afoot, even if they aren't what you were expecting.

SEVEN OF SWORDS

Secrets

The Seven of Swords indicates secrets. Are you keeping something tucked away, or is it another who is keeping something hidden from you? Now is the time to work out which it is.

This card also alludes to someone trying to sneak away unnoticed from a situation that is not working anymore. These attempts rarely allow one to actually move on, so is it worth trying to secretly escape?

A card of caution, asking you to be cautious of your own motivations and actions alongside keenly observing the motivations and actions of others. Deceit is in the air – whether it is purposeful or subconscious is of no consequence. Keep your wits about you and take the aligned path should you wish to avoid heartache or setbacks.

Most importantly, this card can symbolise going it alone. You are ready to discard all external input that has been clouding your judgement and influencing your decisions, and simply do life your way. Authentically. Unapologetically.

REVERSED

It is time to look at your routines, habits and thought patterns. You are deceiving yourself in some way and this is causing the blockages you are increasingly sensing within yourself and your life. Come at this period of uncovering with curiosity, and act on the insights you gain. You will feel all the better for it!

This may also be a time of setbacks and challenges – you are ready to take the first steps towards a new direction, yet there are things that feel immovable. It is time to lay all your cards on the table and trust in universal timing. Often, external frustrations are a reflection of internal ones. What are you denying?

EIGHT OF SWORDS

Entrapped only by your thoughts

The energy of this card is one of restriction, often created by your own self rather than an external force. Are you feeling the pinch of your choices and actions? Or are you trapped in thinking that there are no alternatives available to you, given your situation and life pressures?

This card is a reminder that it is okay to change your mind. Do your best to cease circular thoughts of fear and lack. Acknowledge your truth and feelings, embrace where you are at and then open yourself up to possibilities and new waves of thought. This will rejuvenate your energy, and also encourage momentum towards making the changes you'd like to make.

You are not helpless. Observe those around you – near or far – and watch how they choose to do life. Seek the support and safety of a select few you may bounce thoughts off. Stop buying into victim mentality, and step into empowerment!

REVERSED

Let go of the skeletons in your closet. They are in the past now and it is time to deal with your belief that they define or hold something over you. You are no longer that person. Take the beauty and lessons from them and begin to see these experiences as opportunities or gifts.

You can feel your desires calling you forward and can see a new pathway to lead you there. You are no longer stopped by the challenge or perceived difficulty and are ready for the adventure.

NINE OF SWORDS

Dark thoughts lead to a heavy heart

A card of excessive worry and anxiety. You may be experiencing psychological disturbances and physical reactions such as insomnia, tension or indulging in excessive behaviours. It is what's inside your mind that is causing you disharmony. See this card as a gentle reminder that you are not your thoughts. Simply watch them, do not necessarily believe them. Use your feelings as a guide: they are clear indicators of truth. Begin to deal with these inner demons before your reality reflects them. Do your best not to allow natural fears and concerns for the future to paralyse you. Be aware of emotional vampires at this time.

Ensure that you are not being excessively hard on yourself, filling your mind and cells with negative self-talk and low energy. Take measures towards self-care and explore forgiveness and self-compassion. Love is the secret that makes all things blossom and grow.

REVERSED

It is time to get a strong reality check! Through your now almost uncontrollable thoughts of lack, fear and worry, you are manifesting what you fear most. Your health is deteriorating, as is your life. You must do all you can to begin to get back in touch with your true self. Stop striving for a future that will never come. It is important to spend time in the now. It may be wise to call on the support of professionals or loved ones you can explore yourself with.

Alternatively, this card may come as confirmation that you have courageously battled your demons and fears and are feeling increasingly clear and connected.

TEN OF SWORDS

TEN OF SWORDS

Traumatic endings, sudden change

A time of endings. A sudden life circumstance or unexpected event may leave you wounded and betrayed. You may be knocked off your axis for a period, faced with hard decisions and clawing your way back to stability. This ending often lies outside your control: it is wise not to resist, for resistance may further complicate matters. During this time you may seek attention through playing the victim, seeking pity from those around you. Although this may be temporarily rewarding, long term it will erode your sense of self and leave you powerless, leading to rock bottom.

However, with every ending there is a new beginning. While it may be difficult to see the silver lining that the situation offers, it is available to you. There is no need to rush. Tend to your self-care and work through the array of emotions and thoughts so that the heaviness lifts and clarity is reached. True wisdom will be yours.

REVERSED

You may be avoiding a situation coming to an end because you fear the sense of loss and pain that may lie on the other side. You may feel scared that walking away will mean that you have to reevaluate your identity and reconstruct life in a new way. What are your alternatives? To stay, and fall into the depths of depression and darkness, or to step into the unknown and create a life and future that is reflective of who you are. Trust in yourself: you are strong and connected. Use your intuition.

MAIDEN OF SWORDS

Fresh starts, new adventures

Your curious and logical mind is forever thinking up fresh ideas and new adventures. Your spirit stirs you continually: you crave adventure and vibrancy that reflects who you really are. You hold a lot of plans and ideals for the future, and you're ready to act upon them. Begin to communicate your desires, visions and theories to those who will support such explorations. Yet, at such a vulnerable and fresh time, be wise who you surround yourself with and to whom you expose your thoughts and ideas.

The Maiden of Swords can be an energetic, fierce and aloof creature, who possesses a wit that either charms or stings. A wonderful communicator and spokesperson, she is more inclined to be truthful and honest than sneaky and deceitful, yet she is known for both. People seek out the opinion and insight of the Maiden of Swords, as her frankness is appreciated. Being naturally gifted at analysing, understanding and articulating complex ideas makes her a valuable teacher, yet she may lack the wisdom and life experience to relate to and guide others in a deeper and more meaningful way.

REVERSED

This card may appear reversed to let you know that you have become all talk and no action. As a gifted communicator, you are able to share a vision, articulate information or stand up for the rights of others, yet if there is no actionable substance under your words, soon enough people will see through you. Commit to your word or do not speak at all. Cease opposition just for the momentary challenge and find something that deeply ignites you.

You may be overwhelmed by an abundance of thoughts and feelings; enticed by many avenues, yet unable to decide which to follow. You are adept at using your mind, yet in times like these it is important to anchor yourself and explore the guidance of your heart. There is no point in becoming frazzled over endeavours that lack meaning for you.

KNIGHT OF SWORDS

On fire with ideas

You are underway and there is no stopping you! A commitment has been made and with laser focus you are doing all you can to build momentum towards the reality you have envisioned. You posses great strength and ambition. You may be filled with feelings of elation and possibility, while being focused on strategy and gameplay to ensure you reach your goals. You are being guided to stop fence sitting and leap in feet first! Yet be mindful that you do not steamroll others along the way, and ensure your decisions are not hasty or misguided. While you are destined to succeed, you must consider at what cost.

The Knight of Swords is dynamic and intellectually diverse, often opinionated and electric in his insights. He is very connected to his ideas, beliefs, values and goals at any time, yet these defining qualities are still being formed so are often changing. The Knight of Swords can be a tremendous force for good when he directs himself wisely, fighting fearlessly and often against injustice or for worthy causes. You may recognise yourself, or you may have called into your life a person just like this Knight.

REVERSED

Are you on the brink of burnout? Have you thrown yourself into the depths of a venture and have not yet come up for air? Take this as a sign to take a breath and create balance, otherwise you may become careless in your decision making. Ensure that your impulsive tendencies are not getting the better of you.

This card may come as a message that you have allowed your mind to become soft through inactivity. It may serve you well to partake in a form of study, to sharpen your intellect once more. Watch for greediness and judgement in your actions and your own person.

QUEEN OF SWORDS

Strong, determined and intelligent

It may be wise to disconnect from your emotional faculties and use your discernment and intellectual abilities to navigate this period. There is a need for unbiased opinion so clear decisions can be made. You are a strong and powerful individual who has worked hard to achieve what you have, despite the challenges and obstacles you faced along the way.

The Queen of Swords is a strong and resilient woman who is highly perceptive, possessing a keen sense of herself and a sharp intellect. She is an incredibly loyal individual, extremely gifted in her profession of choice, with years of knowledge and experience behind her. This makes the Queen of Swords a person to seek out when in need of an honest and comprehensive insight into a situation or endeavour. She is a woman who finds it easier to understand intellectually rather than emotionally. At times she can be unsympathetic and overbearing.

REVERSED

Your senses may be distorted due to your emotions becoming overly involved in your decision-making process. It is time now to step back and acknowledge how you feel but not allow decisions to be solely emotionally based.

If you have been passive or shying away from speaking out, take this as a sign that now is the right time to express your insight and perceptions. You are often on the mark. Have confidence in yourself and your knowledge and use it to your advantage and for the greater good.

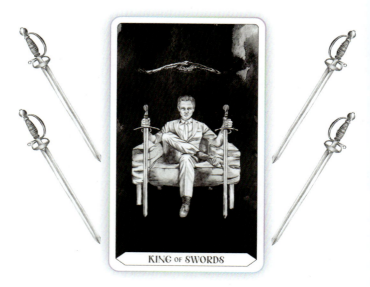

KING OF SWORDS

Truth, justice, power

You are being called to rise above a situation through clear thinking and analytical understanding. It is time to speak out your truth, while staying impartial to the surrounding energies and emotions that may be involved. You are a fair and just individual whom others respect – if you or another are facing an ethical or moral dilemma, now is the time to share what you see as the potential options and outcomes, without attachment to the situation.

The King of Swords is a strong and powerful individual who speaks with confidence built from years of experience.

A natural leader, he enjoys ensuring that the world around him is balanced and fair and strives to instil these values in others. A highly intelligent man, he is able to dissect complex situations and ideas, making them more malleable and functional for himself to capitalise on. Yet he can be devoid of emotion, making him difficult to understand intimately.

REVERSED

You may be indecisive at this time. This may be in regard to taking action and moving forward, or it could be that you are stuck between two or more options, unsure of which is the right path. The message is that there is no more opportune time than now. Make a decision based on what you know. While you can manage some risks, you cannot control potentialities that may arise in the future.

The reversed King of Swords may also be calling for you to come back into your body. Have you become power hungry, manipulative and unreasonable while trying to get your own way? Obsessively micromanaging and controlling others will never serve you well. Come back to your true nature: that of a leader, change agent and gifted communicator. From this place all things are possible.

ACE OF PENTACLES

From little things, big things grow

The Ace of Pentacles is the seed of life, full of powerful vitality and potentiality. It will take effort and focus to cultivate and tend to this dynamic idea. Water it with action and practical measures, and with time it will grow into something of worth – a reflection of your soul's desires and your own personal values.

The Ace of Pentacles is for beginnings, new opportunities, business ventures, investments or the birth of fresh ideas inside an old and perhaps crumbling structure. It is confirmation that prosperity and success are to follow, should you buckle down and devote yourself to the task. It is a card that asks for you to start where you are, with what you have, and trust that momentum will build, attracting the support necessary to see this idea to fruition.

Begin now to inject light, aligned vibrations and love into this new beginning. Each time you do, the energy behind it will grow. Remember, everything first starts as a wondrous explosion of feeling and thought.

REVERSED

Perhaps it is time to take preventative measures or revisit what is at the core of your desires. This is to ensure that you stay connected to your endeavour and creations. If you are pushing forward with recklessness to achieve an outcome, it may be best to pause, take stock and reevaluate what you are doing.

Whether this is in regard to business or personal relationships, projects, home improvements or work opportunities, you are being called to take a moment to stop and truly listen to your inner guidance and ask: what do you want? Don't allow greed or superficial success to drive you. Align to your own definition of healthy finances. You may also wish to tend to your personal health, so you can be the best version of yourself.

TWO OF PENTACLES

TWO OF PENTACLES

Keeping an even balance

You are busy at work and play, juggling the many facets of your life and actively laying the foundation of what is to come. You are feeling uplifted and yet stretched. The Two of Pentacles speaks of finding balance inside your world.

Connect with and listen to the energies of your projects, work and home life, and move with their currents and tides. Keep the balance between your personal life and inner worlds, and your work, visions and projects.

It may feel as though you take one step forward and two steps back, or two steps forward and one step back. Do not fret:

this is what it is like to move with the creative currents of life. Trust that this will harmonise as you adjust to the blossoming changes in your life.

Remain alert, aware, agile and connected to yourself and your visions. Keep your finger to your own pulse.

REVERSED

You are being called back into alignment. Areas and aspects within your world have become disharmonious and you are now being called to address them. Excessive commitments, half-started projects, overloaded ideas, social events or financial strains now need to be reevaluated to ensure that future problems or difficulties do not arise from the choices and decisions made today.

This card may also indicate that you are in need of balancing your inner emotions and energies. Excessive fear or anxiety may be hindering your ability to create a wonderful offering for yourself and the world. Shift your energy so you are not making decisions out of fear.

THREE of PENTACLES

THREE of PENTACLES

The depth and breadth of growth, success and achievement

Many hands make light work – so goes the saying. In many ways the Three of Pentacles embodies this idea. Progress has been made with an initial plan or goal, and celebration is in the air! The inspiration behind the initial idea has been concreted in the physical world, and you are now being called to move into the next phase of the project, enlisting the expert assistance of others.

Trust that you have all the skills you need to navigate forward and accomplish what you have set out to do. Yet know that collaboration is a powerful way to energise and amplify your venture, so call upon those you trust and reach out to others who may be able to offer you knowledge, support and guidance.

You may feel called to brainstorm (soul-storm) and develop plans that tend to your heart's creative desires and your mind's eagerness for action and implementation. This will ensure you stay true to your originality and passion.

Enjoy the success you have achieved so far, and build upon this energy to move you forward.

REVERSED

This card reversed may indicate that more effort, focus and work is required. Perhaps your desired progress has not been made or you've reached a stalemate in what to do next and where to invest your time, money and energy. Seek the support of a trustworthy and aware external party to provide support and feedback. This will create a physical and energetic shift.

Think outside the box and gain a more encompassing awareness for what is needed.

You may also need to reevaluate financial matters or time frames.

FOUR OF PENTACLES

Financial, material and relationship dualities

Where there is hot, there is cold, and where there is abundance, there is lack. This is a card of dualities, especially around material or financial gains and inner happiness and fulfilment. The Four of Pentacles represents your successful achievements thus far. You have generated much momentum and attained a desired level of success, creating security and strong foundations within yourself, your home and your life. However, do not become bogged down, overly cautious and unnecessarily protective of what you have attained.

Loosen up a little, or you risk cutting off the fluid creative energy that has led you to this wonderful position. Enjoy the financial, emotional and creative gains you have made and continue to experience, yet don't let possession and materialism be the primary force that spurs you forward. Do not fall prey to the false notion that prosperity and abundance come solely from money.

Excessive anxiety and control will lead to errors. Greed and possessiveness will lead to loss and empty isolation.

Take a chance on investing in something that would add further pleasure and fulfilment to your life; it may not be related to money, success or wealth. Do not resist the changes and opportunities that are being presented to you, subtly but repeatedly.

This card also speaks about inflexibility and rigid control within a situation or area of your life. Your desire for compliance to restore stability may see you alienate yourself from family and friends, potentially doing more damage than good. Go within and look at what is motivating this need for control.

REVERSED

Watch for excessive greed or the withholding of your love, knowledge or financial position. In relationships and friendships, be mindful that you are not controlling the other – this will restrict the beauty and growth that is on offer. Watch that your own self-importance does not overshadow what truly brings you joy, otherwise you may find yourself isolated and empty inside.

FIVE OF PENTACLES

Learning and growth arise from challenge

You may feel hard times are upon you. Enthusiasm, vitality and zest for life may be lacking, which may also be reflected in your physical health. You may feel you are not receiving adequate support from friends and family or official channels, leading to anxiety and concerns about how to manage this challenging period.

There may be a sense of loss in your life – loss of a loved one, of money and possessions, or being rejected in some way. It may also indicate spiritual loss and loss of self-connection. Misaligned thoughts may plague you and it could feel as though you are swimming upstream. Do not allow yourself to become stuck within the problem – watch that you do not feed off negative emotions or energy.

Now is the time to choose yourself. Stop looking externally for support, love, nurturing and care, and begin to tend to yourself in the way you wish others would. Watch that you do not turn to addictive behaviours. You are being called to address what needs to be addressed. Trust that you have the power and skills to move through this period of hardship, coming out the other side triumphant and all the wiser. Be open to trying alternative pathways.

Return to your roots, to what you know to be true to you, and start from there.

REVERSED

Good news! This card reversed comes as a warning, guiding you to foresee any potential trials and tribulations, nipping them in the bud before they escalate into a more serious issue. Take note of your internal world, noticing how your inner energy and landscape impacts, creates and contributes to external outcomes.

There is wisdom and strength in knowing when to let go of something. Loss isn't necessarily bad.

SIX OF PENTACLES

No one ever went poor from giving

Breathe a sigh of relief. Harmony, flow, generosity and opportunity are all yours. The Six of Pentacles indicates that you have navigated through trying times, coming out aligned and on top. You are now beginning to reap the rewards of your dedication and hard work, seeing growing wealth and abundance flowing your way.

It is now a time to share with those around you. Trust that there is harmony and connection to your own personal wealth, allowing you to act without fear. Notice the balance between what you are giving of yourself to others, and what is being given to you.

This is a period of generosity, support, philanthropy and kindness. The abundance in your life is not limited to your financial rewards, but also includes emotional and spiritual support and guidance – give of it freely, concentrating on your own and others' strengths so you may empower yourself and others equally.

If you need an opportunity, this comes to you as a sign to open yourself up to it and to not be too proud to reach out for assistance. Pitch your passion. Back yourself and know that, in time, you will be able to offer the same support you have received.

REVERSED

Be mindful that you are offering yourself selflessly, not selfishly. Check in with your motives. Ensure that you are acting out of love, not greed or a 'what's in it for me?' mindset. This will only erode the relationship.

This card reversed also highlights giving with the expectation of being rewarded or having a loan repaid. Beware that there is the potential for the loan to be understood as a gift, with no intention for repayment at all.

Be mindful that you are not being taken advantage of.

SEVEN OF PENTACLES

Recoup, regroup, reinvest

The energy of the Seven of Pentacles has to do with expanding your quality of life, making it a conscious act of creativity and art. However, right now you may be questioning if your hard work and efforts are worth the potential returns. You may find that you are reflective, perusing your decisions and actions, wondering if you should have taken a different path.

See this card as an affirmation that you've done everything right thus far, despite not feeling this way at the moment. Allow the subtle pull of the future to wait as you take stock of where you've come from, what you desire and where you are going.

Your vision is of long-term investment, and now is an opportune time to rest and collect your thoughts so you can reinvest your energy into the final stretch of this chapter. Trust in the intuitive leads you receive.

REVERSED

This may come as a gentle yet firm warning to reevaluate where you are outlaying your time, energy and money. Ensure that the effort you are putting in will give a return. It may be prompting you to revisit steps within a process that you missed or overlooked. The reversed Seven of Cups can be highlighting unfocused energy within your activities, calling for you to take time to gather yourself before you make any rash decisions.

Within relationships, this card symbolises that you may be pushing for things to deepen too rapidly and with a sense of neediness, or that you are fearful you will lose what you have. Not all connections are meant to be long serving. Be true to you right now, not to what you imagine.

Sometimes you can pour your heart and soul into something, yet there may not be results. Allow your inner wisdom to speak truthfully so you may move forward.

EIGHT OF PENTACLES

Honing your zone of genius

There's been a deep shift within you. You are increasingly focusing your energies on becoming the expert in your field. This may also mean you're being internally guided to explore and learn different areas of your profession, or to branch out further. This is the card of craftsmanship, where you are encouraged to commit fully to ventures that ignite your heart. You may find your passion sees you withdraw slightly from family and friends as you integrate this new wave of inspiration, making room for it to grow and blossom.

The Eight of Pentacles confirms that you have established a strong foundation internally and externally. From here you are being called to step further into yourself and your skills, embracing them for what they are and what they offer you and others. Know that there will be strong signs of confirmation along the way to honing your knowledge, with success and satisfaction being the reward.

If you are on the brink of something, yet it is unclear what, ask yourself some simple questions. What part of a bookshop would you beeline towards? What is in your browser history? What part of your day or week do you enjoy most? Go from here.

REVERSED

The Eight of Pentacles reversed shows up to highlight that you are focusing too deeply on attention to detail, gently reminding you that perfection does not exist and that your focus on ensuring everything is just right may in fact be inhibiting expansion and growth. Take a moment to enquire what lies behind your perfectionism.

This card may also indicate that you are distracted and not present with tasks at hand. Centre and realign yourself to ensure your hard work does not go to waste.

NINE OF PENTACLES

Independent and free

Nothing brings more joy to the soul than to look around your life and know that you have successfully navigated and created it so fully that it now represents and serves you! The Nine of Pentacles is a symbol of achievement. You now enjoy the fruits of your hard work and wise and prudent choices, allowing you the freedom and independence to put any finishing touches on your original inspiration and ideas. Self-confidence and personal power are yours. You may have secured a work promotion, business benchmark, harmonious home life or other resolution. Any setback, frustration or rejection has been turned into a win and it is now time to celebrate your happiness.

If you still feel there is a small way to go in the completion of a goal or project, trust that this card brings news of fulfilment. Be courageous in your actions and know that your final efforts are worthwhile. Trust that there will be time to rest once you reach the end.

A pat on the back is deserved. Your loyalty, commitment and character are recognised.

REVERSED

Are you working long hours at the detriment of your health and personal life? This card reversed may come as a messenger of rest. Perhaps the overinvestment of your time and energy has left you tired, stressed and unmotivated. Take some time out to rejuvenate, trusting that you will come back reinvigorated with enthusiasm and energy.

This card may also gently suggest that you are living beyond your means or there is a need to scale back on a venture to ensure its success. Do not be afraid to cut back any extras in the short term for long-term success and achievement. It is wise now to learn from mistakes and address any foundational issues.

TEN OF PENTACLES

TEN OF PENTACLES

Joyful abundance and connection

Ease, enjoyment and satisfaction run through all areas of your world, from finances to home life, to relationships and inner connection. It has taken time and effort, but you have great appreciation and love for the journey, grateful for what it has and continues to provide you.

The Ten of Pentacles signifies material and spiritual abundance and bliss. You recognise that the challenges have made you wiser and stronger, providing you with deeper empathy and understanding. While what you set out to achieve took on many forms, different from what you may have originally visualised, it has offered you by far more than you could have ever dreamed.

You may wish to ritually celebrate the completion of this phase of your life. Take time to savour your success before rushing forth. Now is a wonderful time to be with family and friends and to share your wealth, wisdom and guidance with others.

What you have created and worked hard for is here to stay.

REVERSED

There is a lack of security and stability presently. This may mean that your relationship or marriage, finances, position at work or business venture is experiencing struggle and perceived failure on some or many levels. You may be feeling undervalued and burdened with worry. This could be a temporary and natural flux, in which case tend to the matters of concern with prudence and committed attention.

It may also represent that things have reached a state of no return and it is now a matter of accepting what is, learning from what has been and courageously moving forward.

MAIDEN OF PENTACLES

MAIDEN OF PENTACLES

Field of blossoming dreams and inspiration

Listen to the stirrings within your heart. A beautiful desire is forming and blossoming into an idea for you to birth and feed. You may have just come out of a winter period of introspection and can now feel the stirring seeds of a project that requires exploration. You will feel energised, uplifted and enthusiastic about its potentiality, which you should, for great potential lies within. However, be mindful with whom you share your vision, for it is young and needs protecting from others who may be more cynical or cautious about life.

The Maiden of Pentacles may also be an individual in your life who is young at heart, trustworthy, calm, reliable and conscientious with money. Or perhaps these are characteristics that need to be cultivated within yourself to bring your vision to life.

Ensure you take care in building and grounding your endeavour, yet do not be unwilling to try new things, go to new places or develop new skills.

REVERSED

There is a saying that goes: the warrior must take inspiration from what he actually does, not what he imagines he will do.

This may come as confirmation and a reminder that, yes, there is indeed golden potential and opportunity in your idea, however it requires commitment and action. Address any resistance and internal blockages around self-belief that may be standing in the way of fulfilling your dreams. Take notice of how you have been flitting from one thing to the next. Get clear around what you want. Trust and know that the inner work is as important as the external work, and that the two go hand in hand.

Take one step at a time, knowing that you are on the way to building and living your dreams.

KNIGHT of PENTACLES

KNIGHT OF PENTACLES

Slow and steady wins the race

It's time to be methodical and meticulous. Be patient with
yourself as you step into the unknown of your developing
dreams. Pay attention to the finer details, staying true and
authentic to yourself and the vision. Take pleasure in the
routine and tedium of tasks, knowing that the more you
energise them with your attention, the more momentum
and vitality is given to the fruition of your goal. Nurture
the process to ensure the outcome reaches the standard you
originally envisaged.

The Knight of Pentacles may be a person who demonstrates unwavering strength and commitment, slowly but surely attending to the foundations of future creations. This person is loyal and dedicated, often quiet in nature and connected to the earth. They can be stubborn, cautious and resistant to change, with a level of perfectionism that may get in the way. Perhaps these are traits or qualities that represent you?

This may not be a very interesting period of creation, but it's a necessary period. Your visions may be in their infancy, yet you can clearly hold the picture of where you're going.

REVERSED

Have you found yourself bogged down in the monotony of routine, with your vibration and outlook heavy and misaligned? Are you craving excitement, progress and spontaneity? If this is where you are at, understand that it stems from holding an unhelpful outlook towards your life, relationship or project. You are being called to reconnect with your motivations.

This card reversed may also highlight practical matters requiring your attention, that you have been putting off.

Perhaps you or another person in your life is being stubborn, unmotivated or feeling frustrated. Identify what is underlying these feelings and behaviours in order to move forward.

QUEEN OF PENTACLES

At home within one's self and life

You have reached a point where you are at home within yourself and your life. You look at the life you have consciously created, the people within it and the activities and work to which you dedicate yourself, and you realise that it's a true expression of grounded abundance and prosperity.

Often you extend your knowledge, generosity and kindness in practical ways. This will see you assisting and supporting others within your family, community and workplace, encouraging them forward while keeping them and yourself grounded.

You have or are on the way to reaching substantial financial independence through your wise decisions and ethics. Regardless of whether you feel you have achieved financial freedom, your life is strong, safe and stable.

The Queen of Pentacles may also represent a strong and warm motherly figure within your life. She embodies what it is to be an earth mother, maintaining a balance between all aspects of her life with consideration, grace and ease. She may have a tendency to put others before herself or take on the role of the martyr.

REVERSED

Perhaps this card reversed marks a challenging decision you are being called to make in regard to your career and your family life, leaving you concerned about what the outcomes would be if you invested more of your time in one place over the other. It may also be gently suggesting that you have become consumed by your work.

This card may also symbolise that you need to step back and allow other people to carry their own weight and be accountable for themselves. Also ensure that you have not become too much of a homebody, isolating yourself from the world around you.

KING of PENTACLES

KING OF PENTACLES

Final fulfilment

It is important to think methodically. Embody generosity and passion, coupled with steely determination, while keeping an open mind to opportunities that come your way. The clearer your vision, the more power you hold to take it the whole way, fulfilling your creative desire and eventually turning all you touch to gold!

You, or a strong yet kind figure in your life, offer stability, fairness and practicality to others. A well thought-out process will lead to success. The King of Pentacles is a grounded and passionate man who has established a diverse and rich life, holding many interests. He is known to be an expert or hold great knowledge and wisdom in particular areas of his profession, business and life.

This card can symbolise the final fulfilment of a creative endeavour, business venture or life project, leaving you satisfied and accomplished in your goals, allowing you to enjoy your success with the important people around you.

In relationships, this person is quiet and unlikely to share his deeper feelings, yet is a stable and committed partner who will build a stable and successful life.

REVERSED

This card reversed may come bearing guidance to pull back on excessive spending or risky and reckless investments, calling you to put more thought into what you are wishing to create and asking you to look a little deeper at why you tend to go on spending sprees.

There may be a level of laziness or lack of attention to detail regarding important tasks. They won't be realised if you don't refocus and dedicate time and effort towards them.

On the other hand, it is possible for this card to symbolise that you are willing to use and abuse people to get ahead, holding an inflexible attitude while using power and control to ensure you get your own way.

Be mindful of the repercussions of the blind use of these behaviours.

ABOUT THE ILLUSTRATOR

Tegan Swyny from Colour Cult feels like the luckiest person alive being paid to draw and design from the comfort of her living room. She has always loved creating things with her own two hands, so nearly every element of this deck has been hand drawn or painted, with Lauren's loving guidance and support.

For Tegan, this deck is equal parts love, coffee and red wine. It was an absolute joy to create.

When not illustrating, Tegan dabbles in eBooks, art prints, fabric patterns and general graphic design from her home office in sunny Brisbane, Australia.

colour_cult | www.colourcult.com.au